A Long Way from Home

UNA CHANDLER

A Long Way from Home

Matador
9 Priory Business Park,
Wistow Road, Kibworth Beauchamp,
Leicestershire. LE8 0RX
Tel: (+44) 116 279 2299
Fax: (+44) 116 279 2277
Email: books@troubador.co.uk
Web: www.troubador.co.uk/matador

ISBN 978 1784621 711

British Library Cataloguing in Publication Data.
A catalogue record for this book is available from the British Library.

Printed and bound by CPI Group (UK) Ltd, Croydon, CR0 4YY
Typeset in 11pt Century Gothic by Troubador Publishing Ltd, Leicester, UK

Matador is an imprint of Troubador Publishing Ltd

I would like to dedicate this book to my beloved husband John, my six children and grandchildren who I love with all my heart.

Contents

Preface

I was born on the Caribbean island of Barbados, known for its beautiful beaches, palm trees and clear blue waters, this is my home.

My Barbadian background forms the basis of this book. I wanted to write this book to reminisce and share memories about my life as a West Indian so my children and grandchildren can understand a different way of life.

I've had a passion for writing poems for a long time and I've always wanted to share my story with others. My family helped me to write the story and telling the stories in person helped me to document the details which you are about to read.

I hope that sharing my story will give you an understanding of life in the West Indies and what it was like to leave sunny shores for a new life in England. Life is what you make it and life is an adventure.

Foreword

By Peter Small

The author's experience is a sole reminder to all of us about life's journeys – that involves a past and a future.

Una's excitement of leaving family and friends in her home village and country of birth to venture to the unknown is indeed an adventure. What made this interesting and challenging was the need to survive and adjust to a new way of life.

From an early age, Una was a wife, mother and homemaker and she returned to Barbados with her family. The sun and sea life was not to be so the family returned to the UK to start all over again.

Life has many challenges and the author had her share. Coming back to the UK saw Una widowed and raising a family single-handed. Read the story and you'll discover how she coped raising six kids as a single mum.

True friendship or a friend is something dear and to treasure. This is what the author is to me. She is sincere, honest, a good listener and is always there for me. Una is not afraid to let you know when you have wandered away from the straight and narrow because she speaks her mind.

Our friendship goes back thirty years. I can recall the time when Una revealed that she wanted to be a local preacher. I said, "Are you crazy? I'm not saying you don't have the ability, but hang on, why you?" I soon learnt that if this woman has something in her heart of hearts that she wants to achieve, there is no stopping her.

Her book *A Long Way From Home* is a must for you and I. It is adventure, it's romance, it's family life, friendship, laughter, tears and about the love of one's country. But most of all it's about truth. I hope you enjoy it.

Peter Small.
Friend and relation.

My Life Growing Up

I was born in the Caribbean on the island of Barbados that is 166 square miles.

I came in to the world on the 31st of October 1944 as an illegitimate child to Alfred Ramsay and Daphne Lammy – I was born out of wedlock and I was to be the eldest of ten children. The day I was born, I was at my grandparents' home surrounded by Helen and Archie – my grandparents, plus my aunties and uncle who were present at my birth.

My father, Alfred Augustus 'Freddie' Ramsay was born on the 10th April 1921 at Trents, St James, in Barbados. My mother, Daphne Glendora Ramsay was born on 15th January 1924.

My birthplace was a village that was once called Rockhall within the parish of St Andrew – one of eleven parishes on the island of Barbados that is located in the northern area of the island. I believe that this area was given its name because it was a rocky area but it is now known as Burnham Village. At this time, this area of Barbados was truly a rural part of the island that had many miles of wild countryside with vast areas of rolling green hills, forest areas, trees, fields of tall sugar canes, even wildlife such as monkeys would call this area home. To some, it was nothing unique but we could call it home. Burnham Village was a very close community – a family with the Burnham surname lived there as well as my mum's family – the Lammys.

I come from humble beginnings. The house where I was born was very primitive without any running water, electricity or gas. Living on a tropical island meant that heating wasn't necessary but having no other amenities made life very difficult. This house was a basic structure made of wood and had only two rooms – a bedroom (also known as the chamber) and a living room. Having no electricity meant you had to use a few table lamps that were filled with kerosene oil and they would be placed on the table or a stand every night to provide light. The rooms were decorated in a basic fashion with a table and a few chairs. Sleeping arrangements would be cramped with maybe half a dozen people sleeping in one room. At the time we were happy because this was the life we knew so we just got on with it.

The kitchen was a wooden hut that was located outdoors, it was separate from the main house and it had no light inside. We had all the basic kitchen utensils, a barrel of water, buckets and food were often stored there. We would make a 'fire hurst' made with wood, bricks and stones on the floor to cook food. A round metal pot with four legs would sit on the hot bricks and stones and that's how we made a meal.

If you needed to fetch water for cooking, you had to walk to a central point to a 'standpipe' that served the whole village. The standpipe was installed by the Barbados government for public use to provide clean water but depending on where you lived in the village, some people had to walk ten or fifteen minutes just to get water. At the standpipe you would have to queue because there would be around ten people waiting – once you retrieved water, you carried it on your head in a bucket.

Sometimes we would have a drought when there wasn't enough water at the standpipe so the Barbados government would send a large tank of water to the village on a truck also known as a 'vat'. All the village folks would come and fill their buckets, tubs and barrels and store the clean water at home.

When I think back to the toilet arrangements, I remember having a separate wooden outdoor 'closet' which was situated far from the house with a pit that was dug for you to do your 'business' when nature called. There was nothing refined about it but it did the job and we made it as hygienic as we could.

The area that I grew up in was called Rockhall and it included a plot of land that was populated by the family on my mother's side; the Worrells – this included uncles, aunties and grandparents – we lived as a close unit. You would look out of your front door or window and you could easily see your relatives a few metres away. It was good to have family living close by and we all got on well as one big family unit of relatives.

It was in my early years as a young girl that my parents Daphne Lammy and Alfred Ramsay got married in 1948 in a church in Bridgetown, the capital of Barbados – my mum was actually pregnant with my brother Carlton at the time. He was born 7th September 1948.

When I was five years old, my father decided to move us from Rockhall to settle down with his family, the Ramsays, in a village called Bawden – this was also in the parish of St. Andrew but quite a few miles away. Looking back now, I suppose my father wanted to be closer to his side of the family.

As a little girl growing up I remember that my father's family were very old, frail and elderly and they were living on a plot of land in old wooden houses because they were poor too. Looking back now, I suppose they knew they were deprived so they set themselves apart in a place they called the 'Nigger Yard' that was segregated from the rest of Bawden.

This particular area had a few houses, more sugar cane fields, and a large river that ran at the bottom plus there were a lot of cattle that were raised there. During the rainy season the area would get flooded from too much rain or if the river burst its banks, making living conditions difficult. In these instances, you would often have to use a different route to walk to and from the house. Bearing in mind I didn't own a pair of shoes, walking along in muddy conditions was tough because you would slip and slide all over the place. We kept farm animals and cattle that would roam around fields. Before it got dark, I would go and collect the animals to keep them safe – this wasn't easy in muddy conditions with no shoes.

My father's family may have been elderly but they still had small pieces of land within the 'Yard' where they could grow 'ground food' such as peas, potatoes and aubergines. It was called 'ground food' because that was where it was grown. This food was produced as a way to survive and to have something to eat – we had no money to go to the grocery shop. The old people would also keep a few hens for eggs which came in handy and as a family we would often share and swap food items to make a whole meal. I suppose we were eating organic food without knowing it at the time.

Growing up in this area, I got to meet new family members such as older cousins – a lot of these people I never knew existed and we got on well.

As time continued the older generations of the Ramsay family started to pass to the next life, leaving the younger relatives behind to continue their work, still living in the village. I would often get the feeling that being in the village would be a way of life for good because it seemed hard to escape and move on to anything better. We rarely had the chance to escape poverty and earn enough money to move on so we were stuck with being poor.

Around this time my father took himself off to the south of the island, Bridgetown, to look for wood to build a house in the area. We were poor and money was scarce so my father had to 'credit' the lumber because we didn't have cash to pay for it and Father would pay the money back in monthly instalments. My father chose a plot of land so the wooden house could be built – it was a simple house like the one in Rockhall. The first home that my parents ever owned was this one bedroom 'little gamble house' as we used to call them. It had one bedroom, a living room with a small kitchen and a toilet outside – basically somewhere to sleep at night or a shelter for when it rained.

In the house my family managed to buy a few bits

of furniture such as two chairs, a small table and just the basic things that were given to my mum from her father as a moving in present. In those days there was no such thing as a washing machine or iron. Instead there was a large wash tub with a piece of wood as the scrubbing board and that's how you would get your clothes clean – by rubbing them on the scrubbing board.

Then instead of an iron, there was an item called the coal pot which was round and made of copper – it was often used to heat many appliances so it had to be strong enough to keep the heat. You would fill it with some coal then you had to light the coal inside of the pot to create heat. You would then get two heavy metal irons with handles, these would be heated on the coal then used to iron out your clothes. The iron would get rather hot so I would use a piece of cloth to protect my hand from the heat.

In my days of growing up in Barbados, especially at Christmas time, you would treat yourself to a new bed but we couldn't go out and buy ourselves a new one from the shops because we were poor. Instead you would use green guinea grass that was found growing in fields. We used to cut the grass with a sickle (a sharp tool with a curve) then let it dry until it was brown, then it could be used to stuff fabric to create a makeshift mattress.

I remember large white bags of flour being imported on to the island to grocery shops – the sacks often had large red or blue words and logos stamped on to the fabric stating which country had sent the flour. Once the flour bags were empty, we would wash and bleach them white, by hand – it was hard work scrubbing the material but the fabric would soften in time. Once the material was ready, you would stitch a few bags together and using plenty of green guinea grass to stuff the old flour bag fabric – a mattress would be made. I can still visualise my mother stuffing the fabric with the grass as we excitedly waited to see the end result and somehow it did the trick and it was comfortable. Once the mattress was complete, a carpenter would knock together a wooden frame and the bed would be finished – as kids we would be excited to sleep on the new bed as a group.

On the land where we lived there were plenty of animals that were bought or reared from young such as pigs, sheep, hens, ducks, cows and many more – what we used to called 'livestock'. My father had a great love for animals and he would nurture them and care for them. Looking back now, I can remember my father buying a medicine called 'Glabber Salts' to keep the livestock healthy, taking good care of his animals. Having these animals was a way of survival and often an investment for my family because when we didn't have any money we would sell an animal or kill it for food. Often a person known as a 'speculator' would buy livestock from my father to take to market, for the animals to be auctioned off and taken to the slaughter house. This became a way of life for our family – we never grew attached to the animals because they were there to serve a purpose.

As the years continued, the younger generations of the Ramsay family began to pack up and move away in order to improve their standard of living such as moving to a better quality house, leaving the modest wooden homes behind. One way of improving life was to buy or rent land from a nearby plantation that was owned by white people.

By this time in our lives, my mother had given birth to four more children, increasing our family to eight people – myself as the oldest, my brother Carlton, my sister Joyce born on 16th October 1950, my brother Ryeburn born October 1952, Sherwin born in October and my sister Dorcas on 27th March. My mother also had another son who started to be unwell as a young infant so my mum called a friend to take him to the doctor – I accompanied the friend as the oldest child to the doctor's surgery and he died while we were in the surgery. We had to give the bad news to my mum and the young baby boy was buried around Christmas time. It was a sad time for our family and I'm still unsure why he died.

When it came to work, thinking back now, I remember my father's profession was a mason – a skill that he learnt as a young man. In my father's time he used to build entrance steps and concrete foundations for houses. Leaving home early in the morning on his bicycle, Daddy would travel around the island in search of work and finding odd jobs. He would go to St Phillips or St Thomas, wherever he heard that there was a job going. His work mostly came from wealthy white families and sometimes we would hardly see him because he would work till late. In those days wages weren't great, a week of hard labour as a mason wasn't profitable but enough that we could make ends meet. My daddy was a friendly outgoing person and liked chatting to people, so most of the time he would come home from work on his bike with some provisions like a big bunch of bananas, yams or potatoes that had been donated to him and his large brood.

My father was a good man and he loved his

children and we were raised to know right from wrong. If you did anything wrong you would be given a 'whipping' by Daddy – this was using a flat piece of cane that was hung up between the gables of the house. But by no means was he a saint – as a young girl I can remember the time when he came home having had a few shots of Barbados rum or as we often call it 'burn mouth'.

Looking back I believe that my father cared and loved me more than my mum did. Maybe because I was the first born, I found he would be more affectionate and give me a hug whereas my mother was quite cold towards me.

As the oldest, I always knew a sense of responsibility so I would often watch my parents to observe the way they did things around the house. So this is how I learnt how to cook, clean, bake and do household chores.

As a mother Daphne was a quiet person and never said much but was always smiling and friendly in her own way as an introvert. Mother would look after us and care for us to make sure we were clean and tidy; she did what she knew best. Mother was always involved in the church as a God-fearing woman and there was many a morning when she would wake us up by singing gospel songs. Her favourite was 'All may change, but Jesus never – glory to his name' and I learnt this song from her as I was growing up.

My grandmother who was called Helen Lammy (Daphne's mum) managed to pay to send Mother to learn to be a seamstress, sewing items of clothing and fabric. This was helpful because she could make clothes for the family. When I was a girl she would make casual dresses for me – she would go to Bridgetown and buy flour bags that were used to ship flour in to Barbados. She would buy one flour bag for thirty-six cents, scrub and wash it thoroughly clean. Once it was clean it was bright white then Mother would buy a bottle of dye in either pink or blue to dye the fabric, then she would cut it in to shape to make a dress out of a simple flour bag. It used to look sparkling and it looked like it was bought as new.

My mother's time as a seamstress was short lived and unsuccessful – she didn't get a lot of work from prospective customers. Therefore my mother joined her family known as the Worrells to work in agriculture. My mother worked at the Turner Hall Plantation for many years by preparing the land to plant produce like sugar canes, crops of potatoes and corn. The Turner Hall Estate was run by white men and the working day would start at 8.00am till about 4.00pm in the afternoon and you would be working outside in the hot sun. Workers like my mum would even take food with them to eat during break time. The crop season would last four or five months – during this time when the sugar canes were ready to harvest you would cut them with a cutlass or machete then they would be sent to different factories to extract the sugar. Agricultural work for men and women from the Bawden village saw them working as a team with the men cutting the canes and strong women picking them up to gather them in to bundles. These bundles of sugar canes would be carried on the women's heads in order to get them to a lorry or truck ready for a journey to the Swan or Haggett factory.

The tools and working instruments were fairly

manageable and could be carried from job to job. Once the crop season was finished, workers would begin to prepare the land to plant a fresh set of canes or other provisions.

Working in a plantation was extremely hard, thirsty work, toiling for long days under the hot sun with only a small snack of homemade fish cakes or muffins for lunch. During a day's work, you would have an 'over seer' – a white man who would be on horseback dressed in brown trousers and a shirt with a matching hat that had a wide brim. He would have a whip in his hand while riding around the plantation on a horse to check on the workers and make sure that work was being done properly. I never saw the man on the horse use the whip and in a way they were friendly – they never looked scary and I never heard anyone complain.

Once the crop season was over – it was back to the normal day to day work of working on farms which wasn't as profitable and hard work.

My mother's family were all hard-working agricultural folks and that was all they ever knew. I still remember those days when I would watch old Granddad Archie and Uncle Goldbourne coming home from a day's work looking old, worn out and tired. Working on the Rockhall Plantation was a way of life for them because if they did not go to work, there would not be a meal to put on the table.

My mother's family were all Christians meaning that the weekend was a precious time after a week of tough work and stressful days to relax and go to church. I remember Grandma Helen wearing a white cloth to try and cover her head because the sun was always hot. Grandpa Archie would be walking to church wearing his felt hat with his Bible clutched underneath his arm. Even though we were poor, I never heard anyone complain – this was our life and we were grateful for the few blessings we had. Faith was used to sustain our lifestyle and give us guidance in life.

Where I Was Born

I cannot forget where I was born
With a standpipe along the street.
The village school and the church where I once
worshipped
With a timber house as my home.
We weren't wealthy, rich by any means
With my brothers and sisters we all had fun.
We made the best of everyday
Living each day as it came.
We could always look forward to a fine day
Without a telephone, television nor a video.
A meal on our table – we would always give thanks
To have a meal and be happy.
I often think back and wonder – how did we
survive?
Survive, for that was all we knew.
Now and then when I do return
I'm told times have changed
And we've moved on.

Life's Struggle

From an early age as I was growing up I began to look at my life and the lives of others around me and I would compare them. Others had a better way of life, a better home but there was nothing I could do to change the life of my family. I was just grateful that I had what I had, a roof over my head and my family but there was no doubt about it, we were poor. My mother would often say phrases like 'too long honest, then too long poor' and that 'poorness was not a crime' – maybe this was because we would sometimes have to credit food items from the village shop until payday came round again. The saying 'robbing Peter to pay Paul' certainly sums up this time in my life. I can still remember as a girl growing up that I was always careful with money and I liked saving up the odd pennies and cents. It was on one of those occasions when it was getting dark and my parents realised that they didn't have any money to buy oil for the table lamp that would provide light for the house. My parents knew I was thrifty so they asked me if I had any pennies and out I came out with this spare change from a small tin. I was sent off to Mr Springer's village shop near to our house to buy some kerosene oil for the lamp which gave us light for our house on that night. I was told that I would get my money back but I don't think that I ever did.

During a working week, Friday was payday, so Saturday was the day when the women would go to the grocery shops and the men would go to their own plot of land to work and retrieve the crops they had grown.

Mother would often send me with the shopping list to the village shop to get some basic food items like sugar, cooking oil and also kerosene oil for the lamp. The older people always taught us young folks that we must never be without matches or salt. Those were the two important items to have within the home. Matches were to light the lamp and salt was to cook a meal. It was a simple life but I still remember their advice to this day.

Spending a lot of time at home meant I was often the one in charge of looking after the younger kids. One Saturday while my mum was in town shopping, my dad came home from a day of working in the fields. Daddy was starving hungry and there was nothing to eat. He asked me if I could cook 'cou-cou' (a Bajan dish of polenta). I replied and said, "I don't know Daddy." He put his hand in his pocket and gave me twenty-five cents so I could go to the village shop and buy a tin of sardines and one pound of 'meal' (aka corn meal/polenta). I came back and concentrated on cooking the dish as best as I could and my dad was pleased with the results. From then on I was the cook as well as the childminder and I enjoyed it.

The village people would look forward to Sunday so they could go to church and I think it was a chance for them to give God thanks for the strength to work throughout the week. They needed the strength more than anything else because work in the plantation was so tough. Going to church involved getting dressed in your 'Sunday best' – the smartest outfit. If you never wore shoes during the week, then Sunday was the day to wear that special pair. I think it was a chance for them to feel special for just one day.

Meanwhile for me, my educational school life was starting and it was challenging. At the age of five, I went to Bawden village school up until the age of eleven. Children used to travel miles to attend this school. Lessons included maths, geography, English, religious education and history. I enjoyed the lessons and often came top of the class especially in geography, my favourite lesson. I didn't have a lot of school friends and I was bullied. Looking back, I believe that other students picked on me for being poor and not having many possessions and because I lived in the Nigger Yard, an area tucked away from the rest of the village. At the time I was too young to understand what was going on and I don't think teachers really cared or took any notice because I wasn't part of the clique.

I was a very timid child at school so I felt it was better to stay at home to avoid being bullied. I would often cry and get upset but I had a cousin called Diana Lammy who would jump to my defence at school to push the bullies away. If she ever heard that I was upset, she would find the gang of bullies and give them a good hiding to fight them off so I was grateful to her.

At eleven years old I moved to another school

which was in the village of St Simons, a mixed school in St Andrew. I would walk miles there and back each day on the hot tar road without shoes on my feet. I got on well at this school and I made friends. We had to wear a navy and white school uniform and the education was a good standard.

At this age, I was juggling schoolwork with doing household chores while my parents left for work early each morning. I can still remember having to go to the standpipe for water and even sometimes fill up an extra barrel of water – all before going to school. On the way to school, I would have to take my younger brothers and sisters to a childminder called Valma.

I did what I could to help as the oldest child – even though I had a lot of responsibility on my shoulders my parents still tried to make sure that they sent me to school to get a decent education.

The older generation often used to say that as long as we went to school and could read, write our name and could add up sums (also known as the three Rs – reading, writing and arithmetic) then the basic education would have to do.

I was a bright child at school as my father would often say and I do think that he has gone to his grave regretting that he could not afford to give me a better education. As my daddy watched me grow, he would always say he was proud of me and that I was useful and ambitious. He would share stories with me about the Second World War because I was born at that particular time.

As I got older I was missing quite a bit of school – only attending three days out of five. This was often because my mother couldn't afford to pay the childminder so I would have to stay at home to look after my younger siblings. I was always the mum for my brothers and sisters and they were more used to me than our actual mum because I was always there cooking and cleaning. Even when I would go back to school, I would feel resentment because I was detached from what was going on and I didn't feel the same around my friends.

A summer holiday period came and when it was time to return to school for sixth standard (what is now known as sixth form) I told my mother that I wasn't going back. Being poor had affected my education. I knew that my role was to do the household chores and be the babysitter while my parents earned a living to put food on the table so my decision was final. I think my parents were pleased about my decision because it meant less work for them to worry about – a cooked meal was always ready in the evenings and the kids were always looked after plus I would keep myself busy with housework and chores. My Aunty Myra had a son called Kenneth so I also helped to look after him as one of my many duties.

I felt I was luckier than some of my friends because I was able to stay at home and work. So my days were spent as the maid, cook, cleaner and water bearer – often walking ten minutes to the water standpipe to collect water and carry it back to the house on my head. Collecting water from the standpipe was always good fun because you would always hear the latest gossip about different people, who fell in love with who, who did what and so on and so on, I always heard some funny things which made me laugh.

I can still remember like it was yesterday. In Barbados there was a time of the year called 'Crop Season' which was a chance to cut sugar cane, load it on to the lorry then it was taken to a factory for the sugar to be extracted and sold. Every year, many women in the village would work in the plantation fields from April until July. You could earn a lot of money in a short space of time working on the 'Crop Season' so the work was in demand and lots of people wanted it. On one occasion my mother had recently given birth to a new baby so she couldn't go to work. So I was sent to work on her behalf to keep the job for her until she was able to return to work. My Aunty Vera took me to Turner Hall Plantation cane field and introduced me to the people there. The work was simple: as one man cut the cane with a 'bill' (a type of sharp sword) I would walk behind him and collect the cane and gather it in to a small bundle. I had a 'pad' – cloth material that was folded and placed on to the top of my head so my aunt could lift the canes and place them on to the pad on top of my head. I would then balance the stack of cane on to my head and two men would be waiting at the lorry or truck to load it on. Sometimes I would walk for ten minutes balancing the sugar canes on my head – it simply depended on how far away the lorry was located. The average size of a sugar cane was the length of a broom so you can imagine carrying them would be hard work. The warm sun would be boiling hot, beating down on us as we carried out this job and the working hours were long. I worked for most of the season and I was only fifteen years old.

I never regretted leaving school to look after my

brothers and sisters while my parents worked, I just got on with it. A lot of my friends finished their education, their future would include going in to the plantation fields to work for a long time.

Cooking was a favourite pastime and I enjoyed it. For me it was fun and I would cook food like breadfruit and rice, or green bananas and rice but our special meal was a bit of saltfish. We could not afford chicken, pork chops or meat like we have today, we were lucky even to have a simple meal on the table.

As I got older my Great-Grandmother Gussie from my father's side took me and my little brother Carlton with her to a little wooden Baptist church. We often walked miles there and back twice a day, once in the morning for Sunday worship and again in the afternoon for Sunday school without shoes on our feet, hot tarmac underneath and the hot sun beating down on us. This was my first taste of church or dressing up in my Sunday best for this occasion because all I knew was doing the house chores.

Even today as I look back on my time growing up I often thank old Gussie and the memory of her for sowing the seed of faith and religion in my life and taking me to that Baptist church. I like to think that now she has left this world, she is perhaps somewhere in the clouds watching over me today.

As I began to get my own independence and get a bit older I soon joined a church which was nearer to my home called the Bawden Pentecostal Church. I felt comfortable there and made lots of friends.

My mother saw my willingness and my passion for God – even though my parents had never bought me a book during my school days, this time Mother managed to buy me the most precious book of all – the Holy Bible.

Well that book was my saving grace in my spare time because I would read it and study it whenever I could. I can even recite verses from it today and I would not change this because it has kept me on the straight and narrow. Reading the Bible taught me a lot about values, morals and it guided me through my life by teaching me how to live a good life and even how to love and respect others.

My Life

Life, it's not a bed of roses I began to learn
Striving to win the race, I must be strong.
Even though I struggle day to day
I'll say cheerio to those ups and downs.
Life is for living, that's what I'll say
When all else fails, the future seems bright.
I will put the fear behind me as I look ahead
With my mind made up I will be brave and true.

A Long Way from Home

After all of these years, I still find it a mystery how my life changed overnight. To me, I was just living my life one day at a time as a young lady at sixteen years old, doing household chores and living with my family. At this time in Barbados, finding work as a young person with a limited education was tough. Without an education your future job prospects and options were limited so you faced a life of hard work outdoors.

On one particular day in July 1961 on a late afternoon, I was doing all of the usual chores like cooking and cleaning, when I heard a voice calling my mother's name, 'Mrs Ramsay'. I soon realised that it was the village postman who was shouting for my mother so I ran to the front door. I found it unusual that the postman had a letter for us because it was rare for us to receive post. Everyone that we knew lived in the village. When I got to the door I saw the postman in his blue shirt and navy blue trouser uniform holding a blue airmail envelope with a red and blue pattern around the edge. So I took the letter and I realised that it was sent from England, from a man called John Chandler and it was addressed to my mother.

I didn't give the letter much thought at that time because it was addressed to my mother and not to me. I knew that John had once worked with my mother at the Turner Hall Plantation, he was a local Christian man who would chat to my mum about their different churches and he was now living in England. I thought it was just a friendly letter, so I put it safely away until Mother came home from her working day looking all tired and worn out.

As Mother arrived home that evening I gave her the blue airmail letter. Mother seemed surprised to receive a letter from abroad and my siblings were excited so we all gathered around Mother as she opened the letter to hear what was written. As Mother read the letter the purpose of it soon became clear – we realised that the blue airmail letter was to bring me luck.

At the age of sixteen years and nine months, John was graciously asking for me to join him in England with the intention for me to become his wife as soon as possible. The letter was brief, straight to the point with no romantic intentions but just a simple proposal to be married. Back then, it was commonplace for a Bajan man to leave his sweetheart on the island and go to England in search of a better life and opportunities. I often remember hearing stories about Barbadian girls going to join their fiancé to start a new life but I didn't imagine it would happen to me. It may seem strange nowadays but back then, it wasn't acceptable for a West Indian man to court and marry a white lady because of racial discrimination in English society. Marrying a fellow Caribbean person was more comfortable for all concerned. The only difference in my situation was that I hardly knew John. We had never made any arrangements or plans for me to join him in England.

In a traditional way, the letter was addressing my mother because I was still seen as a minor and John wanted to receive Mother's permission for my hand in marriage.

I was surprised, excited and also happy as the news sunk in but at the same time, I felt like I was in a trance with questions racing through my mind and thinking *is this really for me?* I was a girl from a simple, humble background running a family home – why me out of all the girls he could have chosen? Lots of thoughts were racing through my mind about John and who he was. I knew that he had worked with my mother at the Turner Hall Plantation, he lived in St Simon's – another village located about six miles away from me. He was a name that I had heard about but we had never spoken to each other.

Often I had watched others from my village embark on their journey for England. I would watch a car be loaded up with luggage and I would stand and wave them goodbye as they drove off to start a new life – I never thought it would happen to me. At the time I had heard about England but I never thought that I would get to visit the country. There were other families in my village who had relatives living in England – often I would overhear conversations from others explaining how well their relatives were doing in England because they had a good job, they were eating nice food and they had some spare cash to look after themselves and have a nice lifestyle. In other words they felt proud to be away from home and they felt like they had made a good choice leaving the island behind. Despite hearing that England was cold (so you had to wear plenty of warm clothes) and that you had to share accommodation, the stories about England seemed positive because fellow Barbadians were happy and there was something about the country that they loved.

As all of this ran through my mind, I took the letter in to my small hands to read it over and over again because I was in shock. Even now looking back I can't believe it, to be chosen at random for such an opportunity.

I chose to say yes to the opportunity because I had nothing else in my life as I was growing up and Barbados had nothing better to offer me. I didn't have much choice but to accept the opportunity for a new life. There were even some parts of Barbados that I had never been to visit so the thought of leaving my familiar surroundings to go to a strange foreign country was completely shocking. John was now waiting for my decision so my family and I discussed what I should do. My Aunty Vera was especially concerned that as a young girl I shouldn't leave Barbados to live with a stranger. They were worried that if I went to England and didn't get on with John – what would happen? I had no family in England to support or help me and I would be by myself.

Days after receiving the letter I started to get over the shock and excitement then reality kicked in. I took one look around me and thought about the letter and John. I thought I may be young but the answer would be a yes.

Yes it was true, I was a young, innocent lady,

small in stature, petite with a tiny figure but my mother never forced me to take the opportunity. My family members were concerned and anxious because they felt I was too young. I may have been young then but I knew I would not stay a teenager forever and I would have to take this chance. Mother tried to prepare me as much as she could by spending some quiet time with me to tell me a bit about life and the birds and the bees. She tried the best she could but my mother came from a generation that was often quite shy and embarrassed when it came to talking about sensitive sexual issues.

It may seem strange that I was happy to accept an offer of marriage from someone that I didn't really know. Although to me he was a stranger, I credit myself with having a good judge of character and in a way I didn't feel strange or threatened by the idea of marrying John. Maybe I was naïve; I didn't think about what would happen if John went back on his word or what would happen if things didn't go to plan. I trusted what John had written in the letter and I took his word for his bond – I just felt like everything would be ok. This was my chance and I would take the risk come what may.

Looking back I believe life is what you make it and I was ready for the challenge. I felt that I was not going to remain a teenager all the days of my life. So I had to respond to John's letter and give him an answer. It was a simple letter to thank him for the kind offer and to let him know that I was willing to come. I didn't know where we would live but I assumed I would be based in a town called Reading in Berkshire, that was the address written on the envelope that John had sent.

He responded with a second letter to say that he was happy I was going to come to England and he enquired how I was going to make preparations to pay for the flight and join him.

One day my mother took me to the capital city of Bridgetown to have my photograph taken for my passport. My family and I started to think of ways that I could raise the funds for the flight. As a poor family who relied on working in the plantation for small wages, paying for a flight to England was going to be a challenge. John managed to save and send around £200 to pay towards my flight but it was not enough. We still needed to find another £160 to afford the flight. Even though my family kept some livestock like sheep, goats and pigs, selling them wouldn't raise enough funds to contribute towards the flight.

Mother came up with a plan and decided that we should ask her brother Golbourne for the money because he only had two children and was more financially stable as an agricultural worker. So mother explained the situation to him and asked him for a loan and thankfully he came to the rescue. From that day on, I always had a special love and respect for Uncle Golbourne because he came to the rescue and helped to pay for the beginning of a new life for me.

I remember the morning when my father and I got dressed and caught the bus from Bawden St. Andrew to go to Bridgetown. In town we met my Uncle Golbourne who was waiting at the corner of Swan Street for us. From there he took us to Barclay's bank to withdraw his hard-earned cash and loaned it to my parents so that I could prepare for my journey to England. My uncle trusted us and saw this opportunity for me so I will always value him.

Due to the fact that I was a minor at sixteen years old and was about to go and live in a foreign country with a stranger, I had to get authorisation from the Barbados welfare office and government before I booked my flight. My life seemed to change overnight – one day I was doing household chores and leading a normal life and the next I was planning a trip to England.

Meanwhile John and his friends came to my aid – in order for me to leave Barbados, I needed a guardian in England to ensure that I would be safe and taken care of.

John was friends with a fellow Bajan called Lauriston Vaughan, him and his wife Eulene were already living in England. They agreed to act as my guardian parents so Lauriston wrote a letter to the Barbados government pretending to be my uncle who would look out for me and ensure I was ok. Mother and I attended a meeting at the welfare office to discuss my application – the lady behind the counter had Lauriston's letter but she was doubtful and questioned if he was really my uncle by saying, "He's a young uncle at thirty-one years old." I think she suspected that he wasn't a relative. I can still remember the welfare lady looking at me and she said to my mother that I looked very young – I just stood there and froze stiff. I feared that she may reject my application but the application was processed and it was all plain sailing. I felt a sense of relief – the plans were coming together.

Throughout this time I received a few letters from John to make sure the preparation and plans were underway. I remember feeling quite calm and I believed that my luck was changing. So once I had the letter of permission from the Barbados government, the next thing to do was book a date and time for my flight. To book the flight I had to go to the B.O.A.C Airline office in Bridgetown on four occasions. Firstly we enquired about what flights were available, the second journey we discussed the cost of flights, the third journey we chose dates. The office clerk gave us a choice of four dates of departure to choose from: 12th, 16th, 23rd or 31st of October. When I heard the 31st I got excited because this is my birthday and it was like a dream come true for me, the best birthday gift. So I chose that date as the day for me to leave Barbados. On the fourth trip we paid £360 for the flight. This was a single fare to England so there were no plans for me to return.

When the day came for me to leave Barbados my mother prepared me for my journey by packing a few belongings. Mother had heard stories from other families who had relatives in England – that you could only buy items in bulk so she encouraged me to take a needle and thread in case I needed to mend clothes. In my suitcase I also packed clothes that were suitable for the cold weather in England and they were made from thick material, these included skirts and dresses but not trousers because our culture didn't like women to wear them. Make-up and jewellery was also a no no so my suitcase was quite basic. I also travelled with some food items like homemade cakes baked by Mum and breadfruit that could be given as gifts upon my arrival. I was also given £2 (or $9 Barbados dollars and sixty cents) from my mum with the strict instructions that I should send it back to her once I arrived in England – and I did.

My younger siblings were at school so I don't think they really understood what was happening or where I was going.

After all of these years it is still very fresh in my mind. As I came out of the house all of the village folks who I would see around our community (especially at the standpipe to catch water) came to wish me well and say the last goodbye. For people who lived in the local village they were surprised and shocked to know that I went from a housemaid to embarking on a journey to England. I wasn't upset or scared but I felt more excited about the adventure I was about to go on. I was all dressed up in a pale blue dress, a little navy blue bowler hat and pale blue cropped cardigan ready to be whisked off to Seawell International Airport (now known as Grantley Adams). On that day as a young lady who was celebrating a seventeenth birthday I was about to embark on an unknown future.

My father borrowed a car from a gentleman called Mr Springer for him to drive me to the airport. One of my favourite aunties was called Vera Francis and she came along in the car, as well my cousin Diana plus my parents. I never even shed a tear on that day and my parents didn't cry either. When the time came for me to board the plane, I said goodbye at the departure gate, there wasn't much hugging or kissing. I simply said goodbye and never looked back. I was so confident, I had a gut instinct and a feeling that all was going to be well.

On the plane journey I was at the back of the plane. I was shown to my seat and the air hostess made me comfortable. Although I was on my own I was surrounded by other people but not anyone familiar. It was going to be a long flight of around nine hours so I fell asleep and ate a meal. I even remember eating my first English red apple – something that I once had to share with my siblings was now just for me. This was the first time I had travelled on a plane so I experienced some travel sickness and felt nauseous but otherwise the flight was fine. Finally we touched down and arrived in England on the 1st November 1961 on a late afternoon at Gatwick Airport in Sussex.

Back then, there wasn't tight security like you have today and it wasn't far to walk to the exit of the airport. It was a dull cloudy afternoon – what I would come to understand as a winter's day. When I got off the plane I could tell the difference in the temperature, there was a chill in the air. Looking back now, I was quite happy and I wasn't even scared about meeting John for the first time.

When I got to the arrivals department John was waiting for me with my suitcase that he had collected. We were strangers and had never had a conversation or spent time together. I only knew of John through my mother because they worked together at Turner Hall Plantation – sometimes I would go to collect her wages on her behalf and see him but I was too timid to talk to him. Now I was about to meet him for the first time and I hoped he would look after me like he promised.

There was no question that I wouldn't recognise him because there he was standing in front of me at the airport in England with a great big smile on his face with his friend James Vaughn (who had driven his car to the airport). Seeing it was a cold day, John had brought a big dark blue cardigan for me to wear to keep me warm.

From that moment on that day, our eyes met and we smiled as we recognised each other. From the first time we met it was magical and even in that short space of time, John gave me a big hug and a kiss to greet me. I instantly felt that we clicked, I felt that reassurance that he was there for me and that I hadn't made a mistake in coming – my gut instinct was right. Something inside of me moved as if we had always been together. Seeing as I had just left Barbados or 'back home', we chatted about our families, John asked about his mum and my relatives – I think it was his way of making conversation, maybe he was a little nervous.

Being in the car, I was excited about the journey. As we drove along it was a misty, cloudy night and I could see houses lit up, children coming from school and white women pushing prams. I was surprised because I had never seen so many white people before.

My Island

I came from an island where the sun shone brightly
Where the moon and the stars could be seen in the
night sky
I did not need a winter coat nor a heated home
Once you're casually dressed, you're fine.
My island O it is the place I love best
To visit and return back to my homeland
With tears being shed as I wave them goodbye
It's worth every moment of my visit.
The folks there were always happy
With plenty of sunshine, all was well.
Just a shower of rain now and then
We were always happy having fun.
My island it is the place where I was born
Where I grew up learning all about life.
Many years later I leave my island
Making my home in a far away land.

Chapter 4

My Next Journey

1st November 1961 was the first day I arrived in England to start my new life.

When we left Gatwick Airport John took me to 115 Edgehill Street, Reading, Berkshire and this was to be our first place to live. We would not be the only ones living there because the Thompson family owned the house and rented out rooms to us and others. In those days it was difficult to find accommodation because some people didn't want black neighbours or lodgers. It was often the case that one person would purchase a house and invite others to rent a room then you would save money and buy your own place in the future.

When the car pulled in to Edgehill Street, the houses certainly looked different to what I was used to – I felt like I was in a strange place. This was the first time I was away from all of the familiar things that I knew including my brothers, sisters, parents and other relatives – it was clear that I was in a different world and about to start a whole new way of life.

I noticed that the brick houses were all in a row (also known as terrace) not like in Barbados where the houses were dotted around on a piece of land.

Our house looked small from the outside as John took me inside to introduce me to the people living there. As I walked in I felt confident, relaxed and in good company and I met Mr and Mrs Thompson who had one son. The Thompson family also shared the house and living arrangements with another family and their two children.

It wasn't a very spacious house – there was a middle room, a kitchen and an outdoor toilet, there were also two large rooms and one small room upstairs but no bathroom. John was living in the downstairs front room and it wasn't a big room but we had the basics – a bed, a wardrobe, dressing table and a paraffin heater to keep warm. John had made preparations for my arrival and bought groceries. We were to use the room as a bedroom, it was also the living quarters and would be used to sleep, eat meals and spend most of the time there.

As I had nowhere to stay, no relatives or friends – the only person I knew was John so I relied on him and thought I would make the best of the situation. That very evening John took me to meet some friends called Mr and Mrs Lowe – they were people that John knew from his village, St Simon in Barbados. We sat and talked about relatives that we knew in Barbados and it turned out that we knew a lot of the same people. It was a happy time and I felt comfortable to meet new people – maybe because they were my kind of people from the same island.

We talked about John's family situation which was difficult because he was the second of eight children and his mother Doris Chandler was a single parent with no husband. Back in Barbados John had lived with his other brothers and one sister and he had a limited education. It seemed that we both came from a poor background and wanted to improve our lives and seek new opportunities.

The next morning John left early to catch a bus in to town to go to work in Wallingford at a factory. I stayed at the house with one of my new housemates to ask questions about England.

When the weekend came John took time off work to take me in to Reading town centre for the first time to go shopping to buy me all the essentials that I would need. I remember he took me to a hardware shop to buy things like a basin that could be used to wash your face and a metal wash pan that had two handles and this could be used to wash your clothes. As I arrived in winter, John equipped me with a winter outfit including my first coat and winter boats to keep me warm – my boots were thirty-nine shillings, the coat was a purple colour plus John bought me an umbrella and a headscarf. Buying these things was new to me because I never needed them in Barbados so it was a new and exciting experience. It was an exciting trip and as we shopped, John and I chatted about living in England, our families in Barbados and he explained that when he first came to Reading he shared a room with another friend in Orts Road.

Looking back I think I had a mature mind for my age. The experience of running a house, doing chores, cooking and saving a few pennies here and there in Barbados had prepared me for my life with John. For the next few weeks I would get used to my new way of life as John went to work during the day and we would spend time together in the evenings without a radio or television so we were company for each other, just talking.

Seeing as we didn't have a bathroom at the rented house, we kept ourselves clean day to day by having a quick wash using the basin but every Saturday we would pay one shilling to go to the public bath called Jesse Terrace near the town centre. The public bath had separate areas for men and women and we would take our own towels. A friendly fat English lady was the bathroom attendant who would run the bath and then turn off the taps and lock them so you couldn't use any more water. John and I used to look forward to the Saturday bath routine – in a way it was like a little treat and on the way home we would often meet people we knew and have a nice chat.

A few weeks after arriving in England I decided to find a job. Growing up in Barbados I was never lazy and I was used to working hard. As a West Indian person when you first came to England, you would speak to others to find out what work was available. Often you would get to hear of local jobs by word of mouth. A good friend of John's offered to take me to a job interview at a factory called Crimpy Crisps in Winnersh, Berkshire. John went off to his job while I went to catch the bus from Reading town centre to Winnersh with my new friend. The interview was simple and the job required me to be a factory hand. Crimpy Crisps would send a coach to collect many of us women from St. Mary's Shopping Centre (nicknamed the Butts) on weekday mornings, stopping to pick up more people as we made our way to the crisp factory.

The day to day job included a man loading the potatoes in to a machine so they could be washed, chopped up and cooked. The crisps would come through on the conveyor belt for people like me to take out the brown bits and pack them in to packets then in to boxes so the crisps could be dispatched out to the shops.

This was my first experience of a proper job and I enjoyed the chance to do a practical job while meeting other people – in a way it was exciting. In those days you were paid according to your age – seeing as I was seventeen I was paid five pounds and sixty pence per week.

The entire workforce was from the Caribbean, we were happy to have a job and it was a way of life.

I began to make friends of my own through work – we would often chat about our country and our living conditions. Not long after starting work I met a lady called Ruby Downes who was from another village near to where I had lived with my family in Barbados. In those days it wasn't often that you met someone from your home village in the West Indies so meeting Ruby was like meeting a new family member, someone I could cling to. Ruby was a bit older than me and she said I looked so young so she took me under her wing and looked after me like her little sister.

At the factory I also met people from other places like Grenada and St. Vincent and even though the accents may have been different, we blended together and got on because many of us were in the same position of living in rented accommodation and being homesick.

As I got in to a routine with my work and home life, John and I continued to get along well in each other's company but I wanted to ask more questions because I was curious. One day I asked him, "What made you want to write to me and invite me to England? Why pick me?"

John then told me the story of how he first got to know about me and this particular day is still fresh in my mind. When we were back in Barbados, there was one Sunday afternoon when the Bawden Pentecostal Church that I attended was invited to share a service with St. Simon's Pentecostal Church. John was a member at this church where the harvest church service was due to take place. The service was held in the village school because there was a large number of people from various churches attending. During the harvest service people would donate ground provisions such as corn, potatoes, yams, bananas, coconuts and green peas. These goods were donated as a thanksgiving to God but they were also distributed to the community afterwards. I was always very active in my Bawden church by singing in the choir and reciting poems that friends would write for me – I think it was because they were too shy to stand up in front of a crowd so I would recite the poems on their behalf. During this thanksgiving harvest service my name was called so I stood on the platform without any script or notes in my hand and, without fear, I recited a poem. The crowds clapped their hands and cheered. I then went back to my seat and thought no more about it. Throughout this whole service, John was in the congregation watching me but I didn't notice him in the crowd. John said that when he saw me standing with such courage and boldness to read that poem, he told himself 'that's the girl for me'.

For me, my life had changed beyond my wildest dreams. At this stage in my life things were so different and my life was like a dream. Throughout these early days John's support, love and respect for me was always there and I would have been lost without him because I didn't have any family in this country.

Day to day life included going to the shops which were different from Barbados. When I first came to England, shops used to close at lunchtime and there were plenty of new things that I had rarely seen before like an English apple. In Barbados I was used to sourcing food by going to the farmyard and digging up a potato or whatever was there to cook as a meal. Choosing groceries from a shop in England was my first experience of having a choice of what to eat. John would go to a shop on Kings Road in Reading with a list of items that we needed and leave it with the shop assistant. In the evening when the shop had closed, the assistant would deliver the items to your home and this happened on a weekly basis. It was day to day provisions like sugar, eggs, bread and the main essentials apart from meat which we would get from a separate butcher's.

As life continued we started to integrate with more white people. Back in Barbados white people were seen as superior because they were the boss so you had to look up to them. Now living in England you realised that these people were no longer special but they were doing the same jobs as you, shopping in the same places and really not that different, just ordinary.

There were also the trolley buses that would run near our road on Southampton Street. They were double-decker vehicles, a bronze colour with cables running above them to give them power and for a few pennies you could ride this bus to go in to town.

Everything for me was different but in a positive way – I was learning to adjust. I also wanted to keep in touch with back home to let them know how I was coping. In those days we didn't have access to our own home phone. Instead I would write a 'blue airmail letter' that would take a week to reach Barbados. These first few letters explained how I was adjusting to a new way of life, how my life had changed and the difference in weather.

John and I spent more and more time together by going to an ice cream shop in St Mary's Butt and once we went to a pub and it was my first experience of having an alcoholic drink. John knew the landlord called Len who gave me a Babycham (a fizzy perry drink) and I think it was a chance for John to introduce me to his friend.

By this time it was the new year, a few months after I had arrived in England. John was a very determined person and as he had promised marriage, he started to make plans for our new life together.

Hope

I had hoped for a better life
With that hope in my mind, things seem the same
Instead of hope, despair was there
Instead of hope, life seems harder.
I dread to think of that word hope
As I kept on living with one thought in my mind
That one day in my life, hope would bring me some
courage
Hoping to succeed in my darkest hour.

Chapter 5

Our Future

During a quiet time together John told me to write to my parents to let them know that he was going to marry me. I was surprised that he was mentioning this so soon but he was keeping to his promise. There wasn't an official engagement period and I didn't have an engagement ring but I knew the wedding would go ahead and I wanted to be his wife.

Getting married would mean a secure life for myself in England and also for my family in Barbados as I could work, make money and send it back to my relatives. I had no doubt that we could make the marriage work, even though we were young – John vowed he would look after me and he was ready to settle down and become a husband.

Marriage was important to us because of our Christian values and faith. In those days, cohabiting wasn't seen as acceptable within the Christian faith and in some ways it was seen as sinful. If you were together as partners you had to do the honourable duty and get married. John and I were serious about our faith so getting married would mean that we would be respected when attending church.

While planning the wedding I suggested getting

married at the registry office as a low-key wedding. We had no family in England to help us and no money for a large celebration so I thought it would be easier to have a quiet small wedding. John didn't like this idea and insisted that we got married at church and, from his perspective, did it 'properly' with no shortcuts.

One cold winter evening we went to see the vicar at St Giles Church on Southampton Street to set the date for our wedding. When we told the vicar our age he said that we would both need our parents' consent. After a few meetings with the vicar he gave us a form each and told us that our parents would have to sign it for us to become husband and wife.

Soon both forms were posted off to Barbados for our parents to consent to our marriage and before we knew it, the forms had been returned so we could confirm the wedding day as 24th March 1962, about five months after I had arrived in England, at St Giles Church.

I went to look for my wedding dress which cost only nineteen shillings and ninety-five pence with the veil costing only twenty-one shillings from John Lewis, plus I had a tiara. The wedding dress was a typical white floor-length 'A line' design with a full skirt – the dress had a lace design on the skirt with lace sleeves and I had matching pearl earrings and necklace with lace gloves. It was a lovely dress and I felt special wearing it.

Our wedding rings were bought from H. Samuel and in those days cost around six pounds. On the inside of my wedding ring are the engraved letters with both of our initials of J.O (John Oswald) and U.E. (Una Elvira).

So the wedding day came – I was only seventeen years and five months old while John was just three weeks away from his twenty-first birthday (with his birthday being on the 15th April 1941).

To prepare me for the wedding day John took me to meet a friend of his called Mrs Eunice Medford so she could help me prepare and get ready for my special day. A few days before, I took my wedding outfit with my bits and pieces to Mrs Medford's home on 217 Caversham Road.

On the morning of the wedding I went to my hairdresser, who lived on Russell Street to have my hair curled and styled. As I got dressed for the most important day of my life that morning I was nervous that I may forget what to say at the altar but I managed to eat a small meal to try and keep calm.

John hired a car to pick me up from Mrs Medford's home to take me to the church. I didn't have bridesmaids because I didn't know many people but I had friends who supported me. I had beautiful pink and white flowers in my bouquet that looked great.

The ceremony went well and we were well supported by friends in the church who attended even though there weren't a lot of people there. John's side of the church included his friends whereas the seats on my side were almost empty because all my friends and family still lived in Barbados. In my dad's absence, John's friend Lauriston Vaughan gave me away and John's best man was Kenrick Thompson. Lauriston, Kenrick and Esmay Ishmael were witnesses at the wedding to sign the wedding certificate.

John wore a dark suit with white gloves and white

bow tie and he looked smart. It was a nice clear Saturday afternoon when we got married with lots of well-wishers looking on. We even hired a photographer to have our photos taken so we could send them back to our family in Barbados. We were happy and it was a good day.

John and I hired a place where we could have our wedding reception because John wanted to invite friends he had made since living in Reading and a lot of people were from Barbados. We chose Mount Street Hall on Southampton Street. Everything took place in the same area of Reading so it was all within walking distance.

At the reception, friends prepared and cooked the food that took place like a buffet. We had a master of ceremony called Mr Thompson and I think John did a speech.

Mrs Pearl Thompson and Mrs Phyllis Thornhill made us wedding cakes that were beautifully decorated – I still have the knife we used to cut the cake on that special day. As newlyweds starting out in life, we were given household gifts from our guests – John's workplace gave him a set of knives and my workplace gave me a glassware gift set.

After our wedding we didn't go on a honeymoon but we took a few days of leave and then it was back to work because we didn't have a lot of money in those days. I went back to my job at the Crimpy Crisps factory and John went back to his job in Wallingford, travelling by bus every weekday morning.

Occasionally I would bump in to people I knew from Barbados in Reading and they were shocked to know that I was married at such a young age –

my friends were in disbelief and I was also in shock because I was surprised that my life had changed so dramatically but I believe I was ready to be a wife.

The Future

I know not what the future will be
I know not what tomorrow may bring
But this I know is just one thing
That I am here today.
The future perhaps I rather not know
As I live my life from day to day
Spending each moment the best I can
Thinking less about the future and more
About today.

Chapter 6

Our Life Together

Our married life together was very straightforward even though we had only known each other for a short time – it was like we had been together all of our lives. We never quarrelled or got angry with each other but we would treat each other as friends and we knew we could rely on one another.

For me as I was growing up, I never had any particular plans for my life. I remember saying to my mother that I did not want to become a nurse (which was a popular profession at the time) and my mum even had aspirations for me to train as a dressmaker but it never happened. All I ever wanted was to be a housewife cooking, baking, cleaning and looking after others and doing housework.

Soon after our married life began, we started to accumulate more belongings and we began to outgrow the small room at our first rented accommodation at Edgehill Street so we moved. John's friend (and best man at the wedding) Lauriston had bought a house – 12 Beecham Road (off the popular Oxford Road in Reading) so we lived with him, his wife, kids and another family. In those days having to live in a room was a tough experience because there wasn't a lot of space.

In those days we West Indian folks were always changing addresses or moving from place to place – that was a way of life for many of us, starting a new life in England.

During this time I would often write home to my family in Barbados and Mum would notice that my address had changed. I found out in later years that my mum thought I had a hard life and was suffering, when really it was normal to move house often because of lack of space at the property or even sometimes the landlord would give you notice that he needed the room for other tenants.

At the time, John decided to learn to drive – it would be useful to get to work so we didn't have to rely on buses. I can still remember when we were first together as a young couple without children – John hired a driving instructor and we would go to the driving centre on Katesgrove Lane. During the lessons, John would take me with him and I would sit in the back of a little Morris Minor car as his instructor sat next to him giving instructions. John took his test and failed it but then he passed on the second occasion.

Day to day life continued and my life was about to change as I became a mother. Having got married in March 1962, we had our first child in 1963. On 31st March our baby girl was born premature at the Thames Block, Battle Hospital in Reading, we called her Heather Colleen Chandler (we would later call her Colleen). At the time she weighed four pounds ten ounces and she had a lot of black hair and was very cute. We were a bit worried about her but as long as she was alive, we were hopeful. In those days because she was premature, her health was fragile so she had to stay in the hospital for twenty-one days until she was strong enough to leave.

John was given some advice by a hospital nurse on how to feed her SMA milk powder that had extra nutrients to make her strong enough so she could leave the hospital. When Colleen weighed five pounds, she was strong enough to leave the hospital ward which was good. I adapted to motherhood very well and it seemed easy to me. Having grown up with younger siblings I was always used to rearing children and this time I had my own. It was a simple time because Colleen was an easy child – she wasn't sick and she thrived well. I wrote to my family in Barbados to tell them I was now a mother and they had a new grandchild.

During this time other Caribbean ladies had kids of a similar age so we would visit each other to have 'mother and baby time' at the clinic or at each other's home. It was time for us to share our experiences of being new mums, living in rented accommodation in a relatively new country. Not long after her birth Colleen was christened at Greyfriars Church in Reading then we held a get together with friends at the home we rented and it was a lovely day. We had photographs taken on that day – I was wearing a blue suit with a blouse, white shoes, lace white gloves and a feather headdress and Colleen had a lovely christening robe on.

In those days, living conditions were getting more and more difficult and cramped because you lived with other families. I often heard about landlords asking people to leave because they had invited others to stay or maybe the room was too expensive so people would move to somewhere cheaper. Often, when couples started having babies, they were asked to leave their lodgings because the landlord didn't want a 'disruptive' child living in the home – this meant, as a community of black people, we often had to move around.

Personally, John and I found that living with other people was challenging and sometimes you didn't get on. Often you would have disagreements with other occupants in the house about sharing facilities like the kitchen and bathroom; it was tough getting used to other people's needs and wants. John was never afraid to speak out if anything was not right – he took no prisoners and he would tell it like it is. We both became unhappy with the surroundings and decided to move.

Moving around meant you also had to spend a lot of time packing. I may have been raised in poor surroundings in a wooden house but I wasn't prepared for moving around from place to place.

When Colleen was just a toddler, myself and John made the decision that our living conditions were not good enough for our daughter. At this time, John was working long, hard hours and I was at home with Colleen not working. It was especially difficult in those days for a woman because there was no such thing as maternity leave so we had to juggle work and childcare. When you were pregnant you had to leave a job and when you were ready to work again, you had to search for a new job. We didn't have a lot of money, we lived in a small cramped room and we felt it wasn't nice – imagine you had the cot, the pram, the bed, the wardrobe and all your belongings in one room, it was no way to live.

Each time we moved, I would write to my mother in Barbados to tell her that we had a new address and she would get upset and cry. You see, my mother was concerned that I was suffering and that it was too much upheaval and disruption for me and our daughter. Therefore my mother suggested I send Colleen back to Barbados to be raised by her and my father – this would enable John and I to work, save more money and buy a home of our own. John and I discussed the idea of Colleen being raised by my parents and thought it was a good idea. The other thing to remember is that during this time, it became routine for West Indian people in the Caribbean to raise their first grandchild from the UK. A lot of West Indian families were in the same boat. I would say that this way of living became traditional because older parents would support raising the next generation when young parents were struggling like us.

John and I enquired about the best way to send Colleen back to Barbados; we didn't plan on going back to the island so we had to make enquiries about how to get her back to the island. We made enquiries with the travel agent and we were informed about various people who were planning to fly to Barbados and could maybe act as a chaperone on the flight. We were introduced to a lady called Mrs Maxwell who was planning to travel back to St Lucia. Mrs Maxwell lived in Camberwell, South London. We went to see her so we could discuss her taking Colleen back to Barbados and she agreed to take Colleen back. In the meantime, the welfare officer from the Barbados government went to meet my parents to check that they were capable of the responsibility to look after a toddler.

We started to make arrangements to send Colleen back but the impact of the decision started to upset me. The thought of giving up my daughter when she was so young upset me and we knew we would miss her even though we thought it was for the best. At this time I started to back down from the decision especially because I realised I was pregnant with our second child. The thought of sending Colleen to Barbados didn't seem worthwhile now our family unit was growing. Looking back now, it wasn't a good idea for Colleen to be raised in Barbados in poor surroundings; the best place for her was with her parents.

Colleen was born premature so I was anxious about this second pregnancy but even though I was petite, the pregnancy was full term which surprised the doctors and nurses. I went in to labour on a Friday evening and Mervin Nigel Chandler (known as Nigel) was born on Sunday 4th October 1964 at the Battle Hospital making John a very proud father. In those days men weren't accepted in the labour ward so John waited outside while I experienced this long birth. I stayed in hospital for a week to recuperate then I was able to go home.

At this time I found living in rented accommodation difficult because there we were living in one room and there wasn't a lot of space. Especially when we had two small children plus a pushchair, baby bath, lots of clothes and all the belongings that come with being a family. Living in cramped conditions encouraged us to begin searching for a home of our own to buy which would make us settle and prevent us moving around from room to room. Houses were cheaper in the 1960s so it was easy to get a mortgage in those days. We were a young working couple and even though we were on a low wage it was easy to buy our first property.

It did not take us very long to find our first home with the estate agent who suggested a property off the Caversham Road. We were shown around 26 York Road in Caversham. Colleen was a toddler and Nigel was a baby when we went to view the house. John met the couple who were selling the house to move on to a bigger property. We liked it and decided it would be our new home so we paid a deposit of £50 and the house cost us £2,500 in July in order for us to move in to the property in October 1964.

26 York Road had two large upstairs bedrooms and an extra small room that was added on. Downstairs there was a small front room and a living room with a small kitchen but there was no bathroom and only an outside toilet. After a while we applied for a local government grant from the council to have a downstairs bathroom added on.

In those days most of us Caribbean folks would always rent out a room to someone else who did not have a home. You see a lot of West Indian people came to England and had nowhere to stay or couldn't afford the high prices for accommodation. Some of our friends would know of people who were looking for a place to stay on a temporary basis. There could be various reasons why people wanted to move: it could be that there wasn't enough room at their current home, maybe people didn't like the landlord or who they were sharing the home with so they needed to move. Once we moved in to our first home there were times when people would live with us. We charged people rent; it was two pounds ten shillings per week for a room which was the going rate at the time and it was a lot of money in those days. We would often have visitors and guests who lived with us for a few nights and it wasn't unusual for this to happen – in fact, it was normal.

Prior to moving to York Road, John decided to pay for his brother Alfred to come to England to improve his life. When we moved in to York Road, there was a bit more space so Alfred came to live with us for a period of time, being the third tenant to stay with us at the house. Alfred was friendly, pleasant and quite relaxed about life, sometimes this would upset John who would argue with him to lead a straight-laced life. Once Alfred even took me to see a film at the cinema called *Magnificent Men and the Flying Machine* which was released in 1965. Alfred was a kind man but he lived a different lifestyle to John. Alfred would spend a lot of time in pubs, attending parties, smoking and had a few girlfriends whereas John had a family, attended church and worked hard to provide a good foundation for his family. They were a bit like chalk and cheese but they had a lot of love for each other as brothers and Alfred adored the children.

Even though I now had a family and children to look after I still continued to work cleaning offices or working in factories on shift work. I remember during this time I was working part-time in the evening as a hospital ward orderly so I would serve the patients cups of tea and serve them dinner as well as keeping the ward tidy for visitors.

During this time John often did shift work at nights at the Huntley and Palmers biscuit factory on the Kings Road and this lasted for a few years. Doing shift work was difficult and tough but it was the best way for one of us to always be there and take care of our two children.

As life progressed it was a challenge to make ends meet especially because we needed the money to furnish our small home properly.

Apart from work, on Sunday we would take the kids to church. To make more money I decided to give up my part-time job and return to work full-time but then I found myself pregnant with my third child. For John, he always wanted a large family and his dream was to have six children and now we were half way there. Again the pregnancy was straightforward and I had another son called Rodney Orlando who was born on the evening of Monday 13th February 1967 weighing seven pounds and two ounces. I was pleased that all three of my first three children were born at the Battle Hospital which was demolished in 2003 so new homes could be built.

As life progressed it was a challenge to make ends meet to keep our small home neat and tidy. After the birth of our third child, I soon found work again. We used to miss eating the food we ate in Barbados and our daily diet was potatoes, sausages, pork and chicken. We used to go to the market in Reading town centre to buy fresh fruit like oranges and bananas. It was hard to get hold of Caribbean food because it had to be imported in to England – the first shop I recall stocking West Indian food was on Zin Zan Street owned by a couple called Jack and Stella Kemp. They used to go to London to buy West Indian groceries then bring them back to Reading to sell the goods in their shop, which was more like a front room with steps leading to the shop.

So there I was with three kids and a husband and I never even planned to have children, I was happy but one thing was missing and I felt that my life was lacking the spirituality that I had grown up with in Barbados. We needed to find a church to worship.

During my young years in Barbados, church was a vital part of my life and the Bible was the only book I ever owned. When John and I got married we tried attending a 'white' church but we didn't feel comfortable – the service was led in a different way and the congregation was white which made us feel out of place. Even though we had a strong faith it took us a while to find a church that would make us feel welcome. Around this time other West Indian people felt the same – we all wanted to worship in a place that we could call our own. After having Rodney we found out about Abbey Gate Church in Reading town centre that was attended by black people on Sunday evenings. The church was led by a Caribbean couple called Mr and Mrs Walker. John was invited by some friends to attend a service and we liked it. Worshipping at this church made us feel like we were with our own people from various islands like Jamaica, Barbados, St Vincent – we felt we belonged there and we were happy to be members of the congregation. The church was full of Caribbean families who were working hard to make a living, educate their kids and make a better life for themselves. We knew families like the Lowes and Cathnots and we could all relate to each other.

A new church was starting up in Caversham called The New Testament church. At the church Pastor Hastings had a vision that we should buy a building to call our own, for our West Indian community. John, myself and other members of the congregation were given collection boxes and asked to knock on doors in nearby streets to encourage people to give money to help start up the church, a place we could call our own.

The next few years went by quickly doing day to day things and working, then I was pregnant again. At the age of twenty-six, I gave birth to my second daughter in 1971. We called her a Bible name 'Esther' and she was born at Dellwood Maternity Unit on Liebenrood Road. She was a bouncing baby girl and Colleen chose her middle name as Denise.

John loved his children and he could not be a happier man as he saw his family increasing in numbers. I am grateful to God who kept me healthy to have many children so I could fulfil my husband's dream to have a big family.

John had seven siblings in Barbados and one of his stepbrothers decided to come to England to start a new life – his name is Theodore. Theodore was recruited through the Transport for London immigration scheme in Barbados so when he arrived he was guaranteed to have a job working on the London buses in the late 1960s.

For John it was good to have his brother in the country so we would occasionally visit. Theodore had got married and had kids so over time we would try to visit more often to spend time as a family.

As our family got bigger, money was tight but I continued to work. John and I never grumbled or complained and we made the best of the situation.

Work was plentiful and this is why I worked at many different places to get the best wage and working situation for the family – this included working as a factory hand at the Golden Twin crisps factory. I also worked for Tibbers – a Jewish sewing company that made coat linings and also for a factory called Reading Winding on the Basingstoke Road.

Soon the kids grew older and it was time for them to start school which was EP Collier School on York Road in Caversham. It was a great joy to see our first child Colleen all dressed in her school uniform.

Even though we both worked and were very busy our tiny house was always kept clean and tidy but was scarcely furnished. But this didn't worry John because all he cared about was his family and he loved them with all of his heart, soul and mind.

Even though money was scare we didn't forget our poor families back in Barbados so we would send money back to them when we could, to support them.

Between 1968-69 John left night shift work at the Huntley and Palmers factory and went to work for the Gillette factory in the Basingstoke Road, Reading. Gillette made surgical needles for hospitals and the machines were noisy. I followed John to work at the same place where we could work on the opposite shift (sometimes John would work the late night shift and I would work in the mornings for example) to make sure that one of us could be with the kids.

I can still remember those days of us working in shifts when John would clock out and I would clock in to start my shift (which was 6.30am until 2.00pm). John and I would pass each other in the Gillette factory corridor and whisper sweet nothings to each other to enjoy the brief time we had together as a young married couple.

The Path of Life

Along the path of life each day I will walk
With the years and the future so unknown,
Step by step even though the way seems dim
Together we will walk hand in hand.
Along the path, it's the winding road
With many a twist and many a turn
The future I will walk is a distant dream
I will journey on with faith ahead.
Along the path there are hills to climb
The mountain before me seems a struggle
With my heavenly father leading me on
Only then will my path seem brighter.

Chapter 7

Our Life Experience

At this stage in my life I was twenty-six, had four children and a husband. As a working mum I juggled a fulltime job working thirty-five or more hours a week as shift work. Not to mention the maternal duties, I had to look after the kids and do domestic chores around the house.

We had some close friends to spend social time with like Nola and Graves Greaves. They were a fellow Barbadian couple who had kids of a similar age and we would spend time at each other's houses, eating, talking, laughing and the kids would play together.

Our day to day life was full of excitement even though we didn't have much money to spend but we had each other – we were content and happy. Times were tight for us as a family but whenever we had enough money, John and I would send some back to our family in Barbados to help them out with day to day living. Also we were able to send £200 to buy a piece of land near to my family. Looking back now, I don't think we had immediate plans to use it; we just wanted to own something back in our home country. Also we wanted to provide security for our family in case they ever needed land to live on. It was a chance to still have our roots in Barbados.

As a boy growing up in Barbados, John always talked of a desire to become a carpenter but because his mother was poor, he never learnt the trade which was a great shame – I believe that he had a natural talent and would have been good at it. I can even remember him saying that the one thing he did teach himself was to learn to drive – something he was really proud of.

It was a real bonus that John was able to drive because it benefitted the family so we managed to buy a small car. When we could, we could take time off from work together to spend time with the family as a holiday. We didn't want the family to miss out on fun times so on a good day we would often load up the car and go on a day trip to South Sea – a seaside beach resort in Hampshire. John and I would pay for the kids to go on fairground rides like the carousel and we would have a picnic together. There was an attraction called the 'laughing man' – John loved putting pennies in the slot machine to watch the puppet man laugh over and over again.

Once I remember we took our family to Windsor Park to see animals like monkeys, elephants and giraffes and it was great for the kids to see a variety of real life animals and not only read about them in a book.

Over time, working and looking after a family was stressful for both of us and I believe we began to feel a bit homesick because we missed our family in Barbados. After much thought and consideration we made the decision to return back to our native country in 1972. We knew that if we went back to

Barbados, our extended family would give us the support and help we needed to raise our children. It felt like we had been away from our homeland for a very long time and when friends would go on holiday and return back to Reading with happy stories – it sounded like the country had changed so much, we felt we were missing out on our wonderful home, the island of Barbados.

So we started to make plans and arrangements to move our family and our life back to Barbados. At this time we lived in a small terrace house on 26 York Road and we put the property up for sale for around £4,000 and in those days that was quite a lot of money.

A buyer came into Reading searching for a new home and in a matter of months our home was sold. We gave up our factory jobs, we told the school that the kids would be leaving and we told our friends that we would be leaving. We booked plane tickets and planned our journey.

As I'm writing today it seems like only yesterday that all of this happened. There was lots of planning and packing to do as we prepared to move our lives abroad with four small children. John and a few friends hired a large van to move our large belongings like furniture, clothes and wardrobes. The men set off one Monday morning with the van loaded up so they could make the journey to the shipping company in South Wales (at Barry Dock) so the items could be sent back to Barbados on a ship.

It's difficult to remember how much it cost us to send our belongings back but we even sent our nice blue Hillman Hunter car back to Barbados so it would be waiting for us when we arrived. In the meantime our home was sold so we took the money and moved in with a friend for a short while until the time came for us to return to our homeland.

We would often tell our children about our early lives in Barbados, the fun times we shared before they were born with their grandparents, aunties and uncles but they had never seen or met them before. Colleen was nine, Nigel was eight, Rodney was five and Esther a small baby still in my arms but they were excited about our new life. John and I felt proud to know that we could introduce the kids to not only their grandparents but also a generation of relatives from the Ramsay and Chandler families. This was an exciting time for us and the kids were especially excited. We were going back to familiar people and places and we could raise our family in a happy place.

Looking back now, neither I nor John could have seen the future ahead of us. All we wanted was to be with our family and as the time drew closer it seemed like the past eleven plus years of living away from Barbados had been such a long time. John and I were close to our families and we longed to see them again. Would we still recognise and know people, would we fit back in to the West Indian way of life? Would the kids like it and settle in?

Before we left our church congregation had a farewell/good luck party to wish us well – our friends understood our reasons for leaving. Sister Cathnot gave Rodney a toy as a leaving present and Colleen was given a Bible.

So one December Saturday afternoon, very close to Christmas – myself, John and our four children left the UK. We had already sent our car to Barbados so some friends drove us to Gatwick Airport in Sussex so we could catch the Jumbo 747 plane to take us back to our beautiful homeland, the sunny island of Barbados. We waved our friends and our British life goodbye and left our old life behind.

Leaving England on a cold Saturday afternoon, we arrived in Barbados the following day on a Sunday morning. We had hired a minivan in advance so we could load up our luggage from the plane. So there we were with our children as we set off to the village of Bawden St. Andrew which was where my parents lived. It is still fresh in my mind like it only happened yesterday – as John, me and the kids travelled to our village, we saw a lady walking along the road with a bucket of water on her head. As the minivan drove past, John quickly recognised that it was his mother Doris who he hadn't seen in eleven years. We got the driver to turn around and follow the lady who was walking to her house. John called out to check if it was her and she replied, "Yes, it is me." It felt good to be back.

That same morning that I arrived at the family home, I saw my mother for the first time since I had left Barbados eleven years ago. She slowly walked towards me and she said to me the simple words "look at you" with a great big smile. She said, "Where did you carry those children?" I suppose Mum was shocked that in eleven years of living away from home, I had returned to the island as a married woman with four kids and I still looked young and petite – I think I looked the same as when I left the island on my seventeen birthday.

As the morning continued, most of the village folk came by the house just to see us and greet us with their blessings and welcome us back to our homeland.

We became acquainted with our surroundings and both sets of parents welcomed us in to their homes. We soon noticed that my parents and John's mum needed better cooking facilities so we took them to the capital city, Bridgetown and bought them a cooker as a present. For the first time, they had a decent appliance to cook a meal which made a real difference to their day to day life.

Going back to Barbados as a family meant we had to start our lives from scratch. We didn't have our own home so we all stayed with my parents as a temporary arrangement and this was tough. Colleen, Nigel and Rodney went to the local primary school during the day leaving me at home to look after the youngest, Esther. It was cramped in comparison to what we had been used to in England, there was no electricity and running water and living conditions were primitive. We didn't have a bathroom, the outdoor toilet was putrid – something the kids found difficult to handle. Despite this it was good to be back being in the family circle and to be back around our fellow Bajan people who would laugh and chat about the same things we liked and knew. It was easy to adapt to the warm weather – it was a welcomed change from the cold damp British weather but still there was something missing.

Now you know that nothing in life is simple. A few days after arriving I was feeling great and happy to be home but I started to experience some discomfort with my feet as they became swollen. I tried a few home remedies that people recommended but nothing seemed to work. My family were concerned and didn't know what to do so I was taken to the parish doctor in the village not very far away, about five miles from Bawden to Belleplaine, St Andrew. The doctor said I had a fever and high temperature and he advised that I should go to Queen Elizabeth Hospital in Bridgetown (which was an hour away). While in hospital they diagnosed that I had rheumatic fever – a condition that causes inflammation in the body. During this time John was upset and worried – our plans for an easy life were put on hold. I was worried and upset that I couldn't be with our kids – in a way I felt like I was neglecting them because I was in hospital. But overall I had to concentrate on getting better, I took medication and I was under the doctor's care and they knew what was best for me. I received good health care from the doctors but the kids weren't allowed to visit me so I missed them. This was a difficult time for all of the family but I had good support from John, my sisters Dorcas and Joyce and my mum who would come to visit. I was admitted for four weeks until I felt better and finally I was able to leave hospital and attended some outpatient check-ups to ensure I was truly on the mend.

In the meantime I noticed my husband began to feel disillusioned and frustrated with living on the island. You see John began to feel like he had made a mistake in choosing to leave the UK – work was difficult to find, the bus route was limited, the road was in bad condition with no proper pavement. Looking back now, I think Barbados was still the same but our outlook on life had changed because we had lived away. We knew there was an alternative life where things were better and that life was in

England, not in Barbados like we thought. Maybe we had made a big mistake by leaving England but we tried to make the best of our situation and decided to try and settle. Adjusting to the Bajan way of life was harder than we could have imagined.

We bought ourselves a two-bedroom chattel wooden house from a builder company that sold homes. The small chattel house was built on some land that we had purchased a few years ago by saving up our earnings. A chattel house harks back to slavery plantation days when it was built to be moveable so homeowners could design it. Chattel houses are set on blocks or a groundsill rather than being anchored into the ground and they're still present in Barbados to this day.

For my husband, he soon found a job working as a handyman painting houses and doing odd jobs for the business that sold us our chattel house. It wasn't a great job and John only did it so we had some money coming in to the family home but he wasn't happy. After my stay in the hospital when my health improved and I got better John made up his mind once and for all – we wouldn't be making Barbados our home, we were to return back to England but this would take more planning and upheaval.

John decided he would go ahead to Reading to look for a home for us and make preparations before we joined him. One day we went to Bridgetown to the travel agent airline company to book a one-way flight.

A few weeks later, John left Barbados on a weekday April evening with myself and my mum waving him goodbye at the airport. John later told me that when he got on the plane, he cried knowing he was leaving his family behind in Barbados, especially Esther who was a young baby at the time and he really missed being with us. I coped well while John was away and even though I missed him greatly I knew it was the right thing to do and it was only a temporary situation. While back in the UK John stayed with some friends while he looked for a new house. A kind family called the Brankers took John in and gave him a room at their home. John and I kept in touch by letter – John would keep me up to date with his living arrangements and his search for a new home for us and the kids.

A few months later I was ready to leave our wooden chattel home behind. Knowing that we were leaving, I gave away a lot of our household goods to both mine and John's family. There was no point in trying to bring it all back to the UK because I knew we would have to start our life all over again.

When the day came for me and the kids to fly back to England, I was happy to leave and was looking forward to the future. Even though Barbados was home, I now viewed England as my actual home. I think my family knew this and they would have loved for us to have stayed but they knew that I wasn't happy there. Arriving back to England to see John waiting for us at the airport was a nice feeling.

For a short while we all stayed at the Brankers' and they were very hospitable and welcoming. During this time we registered the kids to attend Wilson Primary School off the Oxford Road and John went back to work at the Gillette factory, like before. I got a job at Vanderwell in Maidenhead and I would travel there by coach for shift work. Before long we could complete the transaction to buy our new home, 3 Elm Lodge Avenue off the Oxford Road, West Reading. Before I had come back to England, John had chosen the home because he fell in love with the local area that had all the amenities that we would need like a bank, butcher, hospital and schools. This time it was much bigger than our York Road home that we had sold. It was £4,900 and John took me to see the home and I liked the house – it had a front room, living room, a large kitchen and three bedrooms – plenty of space for our growing family.

We finally moved in to Elm Lodge Avenue on a Friday evening in July 1973. I can still remember as John stood right beside me, he placed the key to the house in to my hand and said to me with a smile on his face, "You open the door." We were together again, happy and ready to start life again. As I look back on our life I always think of two boxers in the ring. One moment they are down on their knees struggling to stand up and then before you know it one of them gets up and starts fighting – determined to stand strong and start all over again.

We learnt the hard way about life's ups and downs but we did it together. We never did fret or complain about life's challenges and experiences. We didn't lament on the mistake of going back to Barbados. With confidence, love and understanding we put the pieces of our lives back together once more and looked to the future.

Thinking back now perhaps it was meant to be this way – it was a costly experience emotionally and financially but it was a lesson we had to learn. Looking back maybe we should have gone on a holiday rather than moving back with permanent plans. By living in Barbados for those five months we realised how poor both sides of our families were and we knew our life would be better away from the island.

What is Life?

Life is for living and having fun
Laughter, joy, smiles and happiness.
Life can be like the waves of the sea
With many a toss and many a turn.
Disappointment, heartache and pain
With many a twist and many a turn.
We do not ask for sickness neither death
Neither poverty, hunger nor pain
Tears and sadness neither do we crave
When these all are a part of life's plan
Of all the things we do hope for
The best of these are yet to be
Health, strength and happiness
We can count on these three.
And that is what matters most in life.

Chapter 8

The Time of Change

At this stage in our life we had moved from Barbados and once again we were settling into our new home. Our new home was based in the West Reading area just off the Oxford Road. It was close to shops, a school, a library and the Battle Hospital and also a good bus route. John always had a vision about raising a young family in a place like this so we had everything we needed around us.

Later on in 1973 I discovered that I was pregnant with my fifth child and on 15th May 1974 I gave birth to a little girl. John decided we would keep the name in the family and name her after my sister Jocelyn.

After her birth I got a job working closer to home in the evening part-time for the Battle Hospital as a cleaner. Life was good and everything seemed to be going so well – John even insisted that I learn to drive because it was an important skill for me to have for our growing family. I must admit that it was something that I hadn't considered – I had no interest in learning to drive because in those days you didn't see a lot of female drivers, it was seen as something only men would do. I was reluctant to do it and found it tough; trying to remember everything, learning the controls of the car and I even had to take my test three times. I would get upset and cry when I failed because it was frustrating and the examiner would scare me. I would say 'never again' but John would insist that I should retake the test – one day he even went to the Post Office to get the driving test form to make sure that I would retake the driving test. Finally I passed on the fourth occasion thanks to John's guidance – that morning I came home and gave John a big hug with a big smile on my face, I was happy that I finally accomplished this achievement because driving would give me freedom to get around.

Family life continued as normal – kids going to school, John and I working, going to church with the family.

The two eldest kids were in their teens and they were starting to carve out a life for themselves after leaving school. Colleen decided she wanted to work in travel and got her first job at a travel agency called Gang Plank in July 1980 and started to travel to various destinations. Her first trip was to Norway for a four day skiing trip and John even took her shopping to buy her a ski jacket. Our oldest son Nigel decided that he wanted to work as a car mechanic. After a short term part-time job working for a car shop, he decided to start an apprenticeship with a car garage in Reading town centre known as Weldale Garage so he could learn how to fix cars.

Day to day life continued as normal, the kids worked or went to school. John and I worked to keep money coming in and to put food on the table. Birthdays, Christmas and other family occasions came and went plus we continued to be involved in the church.

In those days Gillette would carry out health checks for their staff with doctors and nurses doing health tests and research. Staff were chosen at random and sent to a mobile medical centre and John went along for tests – routine examinations. After a few weeks we had forgotten about the test when out of the blue John was one day given a confidential letter by the company telling him that he must go to their medical centre and see the nurse again – so he went.

While at the appointment John was given news – the doctors had found a small lump on his forearm and he was to be sent by the company to a private health centre clinic in Henley-on-Thames so the lump could be removed. John wasn't stressed or worried and attended the appointment by himself.

As time went on, John began to feel unwell and not his usual self. John was an active person who would ride his bike for exercise and spend time at the allotment growing vegetables – we often called him a 'friend of the soil' because he loved growing fresh produce. He seem to keep developing frequent chesty coughs that would last a long time – he would have to take time off work – sometimes a few days and sometimes a few weeks. John would visit our family doctor, Dr Latchford, who would reassure him that he would get better because it was a chest complaint and we didn't think it was serious.

By this time I had returned back to full-time work to make sure we had enough money coming in to the home to cover bills. I was able to get a job at Gillette so at least we worked at the same place.

Throughout the late 1970s and 1980s John spent most of his time in and out of the doctor's surgery, he was on medication to help with this condition but he wasn't getting better.

In the meantime I found myself pregnant with our sixth child which for both of us was like a miracle. Even though he wasn't 100% healthy John tried to continue working because the pregnancy made me physically sick, faint and tired for most of the nine months. During this time, if I journeyed out to the doctors or the shops, I had to take someone with me in case I fainted. I still remember one time when I had an appointment with the nurse at the antenatal clinic – I just about managed to walk to the surgery and when I came out I saw a small lad sat on the wall, it was my son Rodney. He knew that I was unwell and escorted me home – it's a kind and thoughtful gesture that I still remember fondly.

Finally after a sickly pregnancy our little girl was born on the 11th of September 1981. She was a gorgeous bundle of joy with plenty of black hair. Due to the difficult pregnancy we were worried that the baby would be sick but John was pleased and the family were relieved that the baby was safe and healthy. We had to choose a name and found it difficult to decide on the best one. For weeks she was named number six until we made the decision and gave her the name Louise, a name that all the family loved – even my parents in Barbados loved it too.

After Louise's birth I returned back to Gillette for shift work – John and I would work on opposite shifts; one of us would work in the morning and then we would swap for the other to work in the afternoon.

We paid for a childminder called Davina and she took good care of our baby girl.

One afternoon in July 1982 I was finishing a 6.30am – 2.00pm shift and John had started a daytime shift – I had almost finished my shift when a Gillette supervisor called Ernie Stokes ran towards me with a worried look on his face. He seemed to be in a rush and told me, "Come quickly, leave the machine and go to the medical centre because John isn't very well." I was worried and panicked – it's the last thing you expect – I rushed to the medical centre and I saw John lying down on a bed, he was conscious but wasn't moving or speaking so we just waited for the ambulance to arrive.

On that July mid-afternoon all sorts of things went through my mind. The ambulance arrived in the car park to take John to the hospital and I followed the ambulance in the car to the Battle Hospital across the road from our home. I waited at the house until my children all came home from school and I had to tell them that Dad was once again ill and in hospital. The following morning I received a call from the hospital telling me that my husband was going to be transferred to St Thomas Hospital in London. This thought scared me because this meant his illness was serious – I assumed the Battle Hospital had all the facilities necessary to make John better. So that day I got dressed and went to see my beloved John before he left Reading. I can still remember those moments as I arrived to be close to him. He was already waiting in the ambulance and simply waved goodbye that early morning. The fact that he had to go to London was scary; it meant I was by myself with the kids and also still working shifts at the factory.

At this stage we still had no clue why he was ill – I just thought that if he went to St Thomas Hospital then he would get better and being away from us would be for the best. The doctors said it was lung problems but they were never clear about his illness – I never understood the full extent of his illness.

While in hospital, John and I would speak every evening on the phone while life carried on – I went to work every day while the older kids would help to look after the young ones, helping them to get ready for school and also taking baby Louise to the childminder.

During the week the eldest children who were young adults (Nigel and Colleen) would travel to London to visit John and take him his favourite treat; a McDonalds meal. Then at the weekend the whole family would travel the miles and miles to see John in hospital. St Thomas Hospital overlooks the River Thames and John would take us around the ward and show us the view.

In the meantime we had close family friends from the church called Alrick and Winnie Cummings who would drive us to London to visit John (we would often refer to them as Brother and Sister). They were a lovely couple who were friendly and supportive during this tough time. Sometimes I would get the bus to London with other friends like Carson Greaves, a distant relative Ainsley Ramsay and Sybil Vaughn also visited John. Plus John had a brother called Theodore who would also keep in touch to check he was ok and was there for us.

John was in that hospital from July until sometime in September 1982. I can still remember those days just like it happened only yesterday. As Louise was the youngest and still a baby John was missing her – it was his wish to see his little girl. We managed one Sunday to take Louise so he could give her a cuddle. I'd never seen my husband cry before but on that day he sat and cried his heart out as me and the family watched, helpless and not knowing what to do or say.

The time came when John could finally be sent home from the hospital but as an outpatient attending appointments for chemotherapy. As I was often working my oldest daughter Colleen would go along with John as some support. This was the first time that I realised that John's illness was lung cancer even though he wasn't a smoker. Cancer wasn't a well understood or publicised illness – it was quite misunderstood in the early 80s.

When the time came around for him to attend the appointment he was most unhappy and was not showing much interest in anything whatsoever – he lost his zest for life. One evening he had a craving for fish and chips so he sent Nigel to the chip shop – while eating the meal he simply sat and cried – this wasn't the John I knew and loved. At this time John was tired and sleeping lots but he started to lose weight despite eating normal meals. I was hoping beyond hope that John would get better – seeing as he was now home, I thought he was on the mend. John would often spend time with the family, one evening he had a chat with Rodney about what he wanted to do for a job when he left school. At the time Rodney wanted to be an electronic engineer and John tried to encourage him and told me that I should make sure he gets to do what he wants.

As the months went by and it was leading up to

Christmas – I asked John what he wanted for Christmas and he said not to bother. In the end I bought him a new pair of slippers and a nice mint green jumper as a present from his favourite store Marks & Spencer.

Christmas day came and we upheld the family tradition – the first thing that we did was to attend church. John was not well enough to attend that morning so we all got ourselves ready for the service leaving Rodney with him. We returned after the service and prepared our dinner as the children were all full of excitement to open their presents. John sat watching us and he looked peaceful and happy. We ate then watched the kids playing with their toys and presents as we all settled down to enjoy the rest of the cold December evening.

Then there was a knock at our door and it was Irene Mitchell – a family friend from church. She came to visit my husband saying that even though it was Christmas day, she felt compelled to come and see him. John sat and ate his Christmas dinner and Irene said she was so pleased to see John looking well and in good health – she kept complimenting him. Irene kept telling John how well he looked and how happy she was to come and see him. As Irene kept repeating herself, I looked at my husband and yes Irene was right – John looked well and happy. Irene was a widow and complained to John that life was tough as a single parent raising kids – she even said she was considering moving back to Jamaica and John tried to reassure her with some advice. Little did I know that a few hours later – I too would be a widow. Irene then wished us a good and pleasant evening and left.

It was the children's bedtime, around 9.30pm, when my husband started to cough, which was usual and I was used to it – thinking it would soon stop. However this time he didn't stop and instead he was coughing up blood and he collapsed on the floor and just looked at me. By then I started to panic – I tried to make him comfortable by putting a pillow under his head then I rushed to the phone to ring an ambulance. We all started to panic and get upset. The ambulance came very quickly to our home and my eldest son Nigel helped John in to the ambulance and stayed with him on the journey to the Royal Berkshire Hospital. I called my church minister Pastor Hastings as well as some family friends who came to the house then they drove me to the hospital. A friend stayed with the kids. When we got to the hospital we didn't see John and we asked the doctors what was going on. With my friends by my side we were taken in to a private waiting room as we sat anticipating some news – news we did not want to hear. As the doctor came into the room he looked very sad and he asked, "Who is the wife?"

I answered, "I am." The doctor wanted to take me to one side but I wanted to stay with my friends so the doctor gave me the news.

He said, "I am sorry but he died."

The first thing I said was, "Can I see him?" So the doctor took me to see my John, Nigel was also in the room visibly upset and crying maybe with shock. The doctor took me in to the room and there he was, lying looking peaceful and serene. I touched his face and rubbed his head – he felt cold and he was gone. Looking back now I believe that he was out of his pain and suffering and he died happy because

John and I, on our wedding day, 24th March 1962.

Colleen's christening day.
Myself and Colleen, born March
1963.

Myself at 23.

John with the first three children: Colleen, Nigel and Rodney.

Outside Elm Lodge Avenue, the family home for 30 years.

Myself, John and five of our children after attending a church service.

John with our youngest child Louise at three months old.

Taken when my first grandchild Jordan was christened in October 1994. I was fifty years old in this picture.

This photo was taken in February 1995 when I was accredited as a local preacher at West Reading Methodist Church. Here I pose with the church choir.

This picture was taken in Barbados in 1998 with John's mother Doris and her four English granddaughters

60th birthday in Barbados, October 2004. My mother Daphne, daughter Colleen and granddaughter Ciara.

Me and my six children, three grandchildren in 2007.

2nd August 2013 -
the wedding day of my daughter Jocelyn to Matthew
Hawkins at St Mary's Church in Shinefield, Reading.
Left to Right - Son in Law Eamonn, granddaughter
Ciara, Daughters Esther, Louise, Jocelyn, Son in Law
Matthew, myself, Daughter Colleen, Son Rodney,
Daughter in Law Mary.
Front Row Grandson Samuel and granddaughter Josie.
Image by Darren Wingham, real-peoplephotography.co.uk

Taken in Italy
2005 on
holiday.

Taken on 15th
May 2005. Three
of my
grandchildren:
Jordan Ciara
and Samuel.

Myself on a trip
to Liverpool in
October 2009.
This street is
named after
the Beatles'
song 'Penny
Lane'.

we hadn't argued. He had died at home around his family because he was very much a family man and Christmas was a favourite occasion for him and he got to enjoy his last Christmas.

That night we left the hospital and went home to break the news to the kids that Dad had died; all the kids screamed and cried – even baby Louise was crying and she didn't understand what was going on. Nigel called John's brother Theodore to give him the bad news.

When dear Irene heard the news she was shocked but was glad she was able to see him for the final time before he passed away. After twenty years and nine months of marriage John's time on this earth was over on the 25th of December 1982 at the age of forty-one.

Do Not Weep

Do not weep when I am gone
Even though I will not be very far away
I will always be by your side
Even though you cannot see me
I wish I could stay here longer.
Death is something each of us must face
Matters not how old or young we are
This world is not our home
Going where there will be no more tears, sorrow or
pain
All shall be well in that city above
A city where joy and peace will be
A city where my loved ones will be waiting for me.

Chapter 9

Single Mother

The following morning on Sunday the 26th of December 1982 the house was all quiet, calm and sombre without a sound. Rather than sleeping alone in bed, my eldest daughter Colleen came and slept in the same bed, maybe as a way of comfort so I wasn't alone. I woke up that morning having had very little sleep and I went in to the bathroom with tears coming down my face and I began to pray. I started to say the words, "Lord here I am – I am asking you Lord, to take these children and be a father unto them and to be my husband also." I felt empty, sad, lost and bewildered – a whole host of emotions that words could explain. We had to call our family in Barbados to give them the sad news – John's mother Doris and my parents were told that John had passed away.

At the beginning of the day the news began to spread around our community that John had died. Mourners began to knock on the door to come and pay their respects with words of sorrow and sympathy and also tears being shed. I didn't really want people in our home at such a difficult time but it was a tradition and I think people wanted to show that they were sorry for our loss. As mourners came to the house, I asked a few of my Christian friends to sing with me some words of a song 'Jesus Saviour, pilot me over life's tempestuous sea'.

My spiritual faith meant I was in a calm state and I kept asking God to give me the strength to cope. The days came and went as we struggled to get used to a new way of life without John. I've learnt that when all is going well, we can take life for granted. One day after losing John, I called out my own name – saying, "Una, is this really happening to you?" I was in shock and the thought of living life without John didn't seem possible. There was a massive void – he was no longer there as a presence in the house. We wouldn't hear his voice ever again or hear his laughter.

We had to get used to an empty space on the sofa, we didn't hear his voice anymore and he wasn't there to talk to us. The kids were at home with me because it was still the Christmas holidays so they didn't have to go to school or work. The kids seemed to be calm and in a way I think they expected that his illness would prove to be fatal – Nigel once told me that he would sometimes help John up the stairs to bed because he was ill and weak, something I didn't realise at the time.

One week after his death myself and Winnie, a close family friend, managed to go shopping – I will never forget that moment as we both went into a Tesco supermarket which was then in the Broad Street Mall. I gazed around the shelves in the shop and my eyes caught sight of John's favourite goodies which he loved. I felt like I could burst into tears again but I managed to stay strong.

At this stage we received the death certificate that gave John's cause of death as lung cancer, words that we will never forget.

As a family we had to make arrangements and preparations for the funeral but any plans were delayed because it was the festive season. Pastor Hastings who ran our church made most of the arrangements with the funeral undertakers. I had to buy new outfits for the funeral as part of mourning including a black dress for myself. John's brother Theodore who lived in Carlton, South East London came and stayed at our home to give us comfort and support plus family from Wales came to give their support. Family friends Winnie and Alrick took Jocelyn and Esther to stay with them for a week to help me – they were really helpful. At this time I felt that my world had fallen apart and I didn't know how to put it back together again. I now had to be the mother and father and I didn't know where to start.

The following week was the funeral on 6th of January 1983. John actually had an appointment booked to visit St Thomas Hospital on that same day but sadly, he wasn't able to make it. Before the ceremony I requested that John's body be brought back to our family home at Elm Lodge in an open coffin so his body was displayed. It was tradition in those days for people to do this and seeing as John was a family person I thought it was the right thing to do. He was placed in the front room for about an hour so we could pay our respects and some friends also came along to see him. The funeral took place at the New Testament Church we attended as members – all the kids attended the funeral to say goodbye apart from Louise who was too young to be at the funeral so she was sent to a babysitter called Davina for the day.

John was a very pleasant and friendly person so plenty of people attended his funeral to pay their respects and reminisce about his life. The church was full with a crowd of people inside and those who couldn't get a seat in the church waited outside as a sign of respect. There were so many people, it was so overwhelming and I didn't expect this many people to come along. Once John's body arrived at the church his friends were pallbearers to carry him in. Pastor Vaughan read the eulogy and spoke about John's time growing up as a young man in Barbados.

At our side were John's two stepbrothers, Alfred and Theodore, and his workplace friends, manager and his supervisor. It was a day that I will never forget.

Colleen, our eldest daughter, played guitar and she bravely performed John's favourite song: 'Just a Rose Would Do'. In our Caribbean culture it is the custom that the coffin lid is removed so mourners can view the body and say the last goodbye. As the crowd of people queued and gathered to look at John, I could see the sadness on their faces to see a forty-one-year-old man in his coffin.

As I stood there listening to the song, now a young widow dressed all in black from head to toe, I knew life would never be the same. It was a decent and simple service that represented John. Just a simple way to say goodbye and pay tribute to a man who had morals, values, was a friendly community person but most importantly – was a family man.

Once the service finished we were driven to Henley Cemetery for John to be buried. At the graveside more people came to give their condolences and sympathy cards – John's friends helped to cover up the grave.

With the funeral and the burial all over we didn't have a wake after the service because I had enough to deal with. Now was the time for me to consider the future for me and the six children. With most of our family living in Barbados, I didn't have family support or anyone to help with day to day family life. There wasn't time to sit and feel sorry for myself and I wasn't angry with God. Time was very precious and I had my children which was the most important thing to me then and still is.

After John's funeral on 6th January 1983, my family and I went to church on Sunday 8th January and John's brother Alfred also joined us at church for support. Alrick our family friend offered to drive us to church which was a kind offer but as the new head of the family, I decided to take charge and drive my six children to church on that Sunday morning. After all, what else could I do?

That first day back at church is still fresh in my mind. As I entered the building, the congregation was singing, shouting and clapping their hands and worshipping as normal. There I was, dressed from head to toe in black with a veil to try and hide the tears flowing down my face, cradling my baby in my arms. The seat where John would normally sit in church was empty.

Though I felt the pain and the hurt of grief I tried to stay strong for my young family's sake. The person who I and the children once knew as Dad was no longer there but for his sake we had to carry on – this was what he would have wanted. After the funeral my mother called from Barbados to see how I was coping because the family were worried about me. I told my mother to give a message to our family: do not pity me, just keep praying that God will give me strength to go on.

Single Mother

Just like so many others in this world
I never chose to be a single parent
Looking after a family has its ups and downs
Troubles and trials, fun and laughter
So come on all you single parents
Life can be fun even though it may be tough
Let's show our children how much we do love them
Even when the pain is hurting come on let us be
Happy and enjoy our children.

Chapter 10

Alone but Not Alone

After John's funeral we tried to get back to normal as much as possible. The children went back to junior school and the older kids went back to work leaving me and Louise at home. People would often ask me, "How did you cope?" Growing up in Barbados with no money, no luxury and just a few friends gave me the experience to deal with tough situations. My life as a wife was over but my work as a parent was just starting.

Just weeks after losing John, the family car that was parked outside the house was involved in an accident. Someone had driven in to it and caused damage to the wing of the car. This was the first experience I had of coping with life as a single mum and coping with life by myself. I didn't have John to turn to for advice. I now had to deal with things by myself as the head of the family with the kids for support.

I had the responsibility of running and maintaining a home, performing the role of mum and dad, paying the bills and driving the kids around. If one of the children had an appointment at the hospital, doctor or dentist it was useful to be able to drive to get around. I didn't return back to work at the Gillette factory – I handed in my notice. The thought of juggling childcare, running a home and looking after my family would be too much to bear plus grieving was taking its toll. Emotionally and physically I didn't have the strength to juggle work in addition to everything else. Yes – we needed the money but losing John had taught me that family life was more important and I needed to be around for the kids more than ever. I never regretted leaving that job because I felt it was important to be around for the children.

My Christian faith played a very important role in my life – my daily routine always included a prayer before my household duties. It would be a prayer to give me strength, I would make sure the kids were ready to go to school; the older kids would leave for work and baby Louise would be left at home. I would do the housework, do the washing to make sure the kids had clean clothes, and go food shopping and all the other day to day chores. John would always sweep the yard, clean the windows and clean out the drains but now these were part of my duties on top of everything else.

John was well known within the community so it seemed like people were speculating and gossiping about why he died. I would bump into family friends around the town centre and they would tell me about rumours they had heard about John and why he had died. People were suggesting that I had played a part in his death. I suppose in those days, cancer was a rare illness and people were ignorant to the illness so speculation was rife. Hearing the rumours was upsetting and hurtful – I expected support from the community not gossip. It made me feel upset and I became guarded because I didn't know if people were genuine when they were asking questions or were they spreading lies? People expected me to walk the streets crying and being openly upset but I stayed strong. Now I was the head of the family so I sat the children down and I gave them some advice. I told them, "Do not walk the streets and let people see you crying on the roads. Come home and let us close the door and cry together to support each other." I didn't want to give the black community a reason to spread more rumours about us, we had to stay strong. The kids listened to me and did what they were told to keep the unkind words and gossip at bay. Now the years have passed, my kids still remember these words and they thanked me for being so strong.

When John was alive, he had an allotment on Scours Lane in Reading that cost £6 per year – it was his pride and joy growing vegetables, potatoes, onions, marrows and carrots. I think it was a way to connect with his Caribbean roots of growing food items like when he was a young boy in Barbados. I remember the day when I went to Reading Borough Council to hand back the ownership of the allotment. At the time, the receptionist looked so sad when I told her the reason for handing back the keys so someone else could have his patch.

Each morning before I began my day, I would always read the Bible psalm 121, 'I lift my eyes unto the hills from whence my help cometh'. These words gave me great strength and courage to keep going during these dark days – I suppose these words inspired me and gave me comfort.

During this phase of grieving I would sit during the mid-morning and read my Bible and when I opened the King James version, I saw Jeremiah chapter 29 v 11. There is a verse that says, 'For I know the plans I have for you, plans for good and not for evil to give you a future and a hope. In those days when you pray, I will listen'. As I read these words, it brought a kind of peace and comfort knowing that God was watching over me.

I quickly found myself reading the words: 'For I know the thoughts that I think toward you, saith the Lord, thoughts of peace and not of evil, to give you an expected end'.

Reading these words – I had a breakthrough in my mind. It was like it was a sign for my grief to fade, it gave me assurance that someone was with me and I had the presence of God to give me strength to carry on. My tears disappeared.

Nothing could take away the pain and grief. I missed John so much but I had to find a way to cope, to get through the days, weeks and months. It was a matter of sink or swim and I owed it to John's legacy to raise his kids and do my best now he wasn't around.

Something else happened a few months after John's death. I was all alone at home and in the kitchen I saw before my eyes a ladder and I heard an invisible voice calling out to me, saying, "Look there is a ladder – step on it and climb, and go forward." When I heard these words, I felt great, I wasn't scared or anything and from that day my tears started to dry up. These simple words gave me courage and confidence, shook me from my grief and gave me the determination to never look back.

I began to realise that whatever was happening in my life, God was in control and that brought a great feeling of peace and joy.

At this stage, I decided to go back to Barbados and visit my family for a break. Since John had died my family were worried about me and how I would cope so I decided to take the youngest three kids back to Barbados for four weeks. It would give me a chance to see my family, John's family and for the kids to see their relatives. Going back now was different in many ways – the last time I was on the island was ten years ago with John and our four kids. Now I was making the trip as a single mother of six kids. Despite the sadness, the trip was enjoyable and it was nice to be back around my family. The kids got a chance to spend time with their aunties and uncles and grandparents which are memories they still treasure to this day.

I began to feel the strength, courage and confidence as I told myself that someone, somewhere was surely praying and looking over me and maybe I wasn't alone after all.

Feeling Sad

When you are feeling sad and lonely
Bent beneath with a load of care
Just remember that there is a God in heaven
Who is beside you even then
God will never, never leave you
Every moment he is with you
Just be still and give him some time
Wait with patience, watch and pray.

Chapter 11

Finding My Own Way

I now had to take each day at a time. I was on my own and didn't have a lot of contact with my family in Barbados apart from letters. As a family we were all adjusting to life without John. I was on a journey and I had no clue where to start or where the path of life would take me.

The time came for us to tidy through John's clothes. We couldn't keep them forever and it took a lot of strength for me to even think about giving them away. One day I was looking at the local newspaper and a charity shop called Keep near to the Brook Barracks was advertising for men's clothes. I folded up John's clothes and I took them there. As I was going through the trousers, in the pocket I found his handkerchiefs, cough sweets and tissues – all the things that reminded me of him. I did keep John's trilby hat which I still have to this day.

The kids were trying to adjust to life without a dad. They were quiet and trying to get back to normal as much as possible by going to school and work. I know it wasn't easy for them but at least we had each other.

My days felt empty and strange without John.

During these early days I would try and fill my days. Louise my youngest daughter became my companion during the day to keep me company. Sometimes I would get lonely in the house so I would put Lou in her buggy and go for a gentle walk in to the town centre to browse around the shops for something to do. I would then return home in time to greet Esther and Jocelyn from school which helped to ease the pain of being lonely.

As a family we went on with life and the day to day duties. I wondered what I could do next to occupy my time and my first thought was to do some voluntary work within my community. I was widowed at the age of thirty-eight but I still felt I had something to offer the community. Paid work wasn't really an option because I had my young family to look after and nurture. Voluntary work seemed like a nice flexible way for me to give something back to the healthcare system who cared for John during his illness. I have always been an active person and I was looking for something to fill my spare time. Now I was a single mother and housewife, I was responsible for looking after my family but voluntary work could provide me with a way to keep active, meet people and give me a sense of responsibility and routine in my life – something that I missed.

At this stage, I noticed a sign at 125 Oxford Road for a bereavement support group called 'Cruse'. I was curious to know what they did so I decided to pop in. Every Monday morning I would sit in with a group of grieving ladies as we came to terms with life without our husbands. We all cried together, understood how each other felt and could offer words of encouragement and support over a cup of tea. Over the years, Cruse would organise activities and outings for us and our kids at Christmas time, daytrips and a holiday to Dorset at a caravan park. Cruse played such an important part in my life at this time to help me back on to my feet. It was a chance for me to start being normal again and get back to some sort of routine.

One day I was reading our local newspaper and I noticed an advert for the local Citizens Advice Bureau, they were searching for volunteer workers to work in their office. I thought I should take up the offer and applied for the position. Sooner than later I was sent an application form which I completed and returned, feeling anxious and not knowing what would happen next.

It was about four months after John's death that I was given a date for the interview and it took place on a cold afternoon. I got dressed and took my baby in my arms and went along to the CAB office which was situated in St. Mary's Butts. I entered a very large old building with plenty of steps and it was very cold inside.

As I reached the entrance and rang the bell – a lady came and introduced herself as Joan Rudduck. I told her I had an appointment to find out about voluntary work as she made me welcome with a cup of tea.

We sat and chatted about my life and I described why I was applying for voluntary work. To my amazement Joan explained that she could not accept me as a volunteer because I would have to attend training courses and I couldn't do this while also caring for a young family who depended on me.

I was disappointed but she gave me some good news – before I left her office that afternoon she said to me, "I'm going to see what I can do," and she wrote down an address for another volunteer centre on Parkside Road, Reading.

When I left the office that afternoon, I felt happy and reassured that something good was coming my way and I could be useful to someone. When I went to leave Joan's office she said, "I think you're going to do well." These positive words were comforting – it was good to know that someone had faith in me.

In the meantime, as Louise got a little bit older she was ready to be accepted in to Wilson Nursery School. The head mistress Mrs Tucker knew my family well (Esther and Jocelyn already attended the school) so she agreed to let Louise attend the nursery a bit earlier than planned, to give me a break – as a sign of compassion.

What Jo Tucker did for me was like an answer to my prayers – it gave me flexibility with my day to pursue the volunteering. I went back to the volunteer centre on Parkside Road and signed up to be a volunteer.

When I looked at the address for the volunteer centre, I had never heard of it before, even though I had lived in Reading for many years. I was curious and determined to find the location so I went to find it the following day. As I approached the entrance door I rang the bell and a lady answered – I explained that I was there to be a volunteer. At the time it didn't matter what I did as a volunteer, I just wanted to help.

As I went inside I was made welcome and I noticed it was a pleasant place that was very quiet.

A member of staff began to show me a list that outlined all of the different ways that I could help and I could choose. I could befriend elderly people at their home or maybe visit elderly people in residential care homes.

I noticed on the list that a residential care home next door called Rose Lawn needed volunteers to visit the elderly so I decided to go for it. The volunteer worker was pleased that I had chosen this role and she thought it was strange that someone of thirty-nine years old wanted to volunteer and not do paid work. I explained to her my circumstances and she was pleased to sign me up. I would often take Louise in to nursery school then walk about twenty minutes to the care home.

I started the voluntary work on a trial basis because I wasn't sure if I would like it and I didn't know what to expect. The position I accepted meant I could visit the care home two afternoons a week to serve tea and chat to the elderly and listen to them as they reminisced about their lives. People living at Rose Lawn were frail and sometimes sick so I would read to them and keep them company. I remember befriending a lady called Vera from Knotty Ash in Liverpool and she told me about her husband who worked hard and how they saved money and he had died. I was able to understand how she felt and I found it rewarding to know that she could confide in me. Volunteering at Rose Lawn helped to take my mind off my grief and missing John but I was happy because I felt that I was doing something that I loved and enjoyed.

As time passed I began to feel more confident in myself and I soon felt that I wanted to do more volunteer work. I heard about the Red Cross Centre in Tilehurst that wanted volunteers to learn first aid. I learnt how to do bandages, how to tend to grazes, cuts and injuries and these were all things that were handy to know when you're a mother of a young family. Looking back now it was a chance to learn resuscitation skills that could have saved John's life and even though it was too late and he was gone, I thought it was worthwhile to learn first aid.

Every Thursday evening I would prepare dinner for the kids so they had a meal when they came home from work and school then I would go out to my class. I enjoyed meeting other people and it was interesting to learn new things about health and safety. I had a uniform: a navy blue skirt, long-sleeved white blouse and a navy blue beret with a Red Cross badge. I made a few friends at the class and I would go on social events with ladies like Mrs French the first aid leader. As a team we would sometimes go out on Red Cross duties to give medical assistance at events like fetes and we accompanied elderly people on a day trip to Southsea. I even bought books to learn more about first aid and I had to study for exams and I passed them. The first aid sessions gave me a chance to get out of the house and be more than a mother and a housewife – it was doing something I enjoyed.

I was now carving out a new life for myself and I was on a journey – I never made any plans. I simply relied on my instinct and confidence to get by.

Onward and Upward

Onward and upward each day as I walk
With my head held high and my feet on the ground
Ready, steady onward I will go
With a made up mind and nothing to fear.

Chapter 12

Being Myself

At this stage in my life I was slowly coming to terms with my loss but my faith was still important to me. After John's death I continued to worship at the New Testament Church in Caversham – I would drive there every Sunday morning and evening for the weekly service, taking the kids with me because it was my spiritual home. As a family we worshipped at this church for fifteen years – we had made many friends and formed a strong bond with a network of people who would help each other during times of need. I was brought up in the Pentecostal Church and was familiar with the style of worship – it made me feel safe to be there because I found comfort, warmth and fellowship to be with people of my own kind.

When I first came to England it was widely said that English white churches didn't always welcome black worshippers so it was good to be somewhere where you felt you belonged. Looking back now, we were all in the same boat, living day to day, working, raising a family and having a social bond through the church. It was a place that was familiar to us.

As a church we used to go out on outings

together to different towns and cities, we went to places like Wolverhampton, Leicester and Aylesbury, these were called conventions and they allowed different churches to come together at one place.

Dealing with grief and challenging times I expected the church and the congregation to support myself and the kids – after all these people knew us best and could provide the comfort that we needed. However after some time I began to notice that though I was surrounded by a large congregation of Christians, somehow I began feeling a sense of loneliness and rejection. It felt like people weren't talking to me and we felt ostracised and I began to question my faith and my desire for God in my life. Maybe the church congregation were unsure of what to say or didn't know how to address grief but they never phoned or visited our family home. As members of the congregation in the church we referred to each other as 'brother' and 'sister'. This was a way of feeling like we were equal and living as one big Christian community. I expected more from the my 'brothers' and 'sisters' – support, guidance or some comforting words from the people I knew so well and respected. Instead I felt like I was left out in the cold. We were just left to our own devices to get on with it and I was upset and shocked.

It was a very difficult time for me and I wondered what I could do next. I didn't do anything spontaneous or rash – I decided that I would spend much of my time praying and seeking advice from God for the right direction for my life.

It was 1984 and one night, while I was asleep, I believe that God visited me in a dream and I saw a vision of myself standing outside the West Reading Methodist Church. In those days when we lived at Elm Lodge Avenue, the West Reading Methodist Church was around the corner and across the road from our home. The dream had confirmed that it was time to move on and I wasn't scared or daunted.

I woke up the next morning and decided that I would visit and get a feel of the church, the people and the style of worship. I also told my daughter Colleen that God was showing me where to worship. Soon after I wrote a letter to Pastor Lawrence to tell him I had decided to take my membership to the Methodist Church and leave the New Testament Church behind and I got no response or acknowledgement, confirming it was time to move on.

I told the kids what was going on and I didn't stop the kids from continuing at our family church – for a while Colleen would drive the four kids to attend service but soon the visits fizzled out. The only person that came with me to the Methodist services was Louise because she was the youngest and she needed my care.

I remember the first time I attended the Methodist Church, it was evening service. It was strange at first because I didn't know a lot of people there and everything was new but I knew that what I was doing was right. Even though all the familiar people that I knew were not there for me, I maintained my faith and trust in God. I noticed that people greeted me and seemed happy to see me. I noticed that the style of worship was different – it wasn't as lively or charismatic, it always ran to time and the service was conducted in an organised fashion with a structure. The hymns and singing were more reserved but I was happy to be in their presence. I remember meeting congregation members David Geary, David Hull and Gordon Wilson – the minister at the time was a lady called Pat Ing and they all made me feel welcome.

Weeks passed and I decided that I would like to be a member of the Methodist Church – so Pat Ing came to my home to have a chat then she encouraged me to attend classes that would explain the Methodist style of worship. I agreed to attend the classes at Pat's home along with a few other people to learn the teachings of the Methodist Church and it confirmed that this was the place for me to be.

A month later, I attended a Sunday evening service as normal and was called to the pulpit to take a vow of membership to be accepted as an official member of the congregation – I felt happy and accepted and ready to start my new life being me.

Myself

Of all the things that I love to be
I love to be me
No one can take this away from me
I am only too proud to be the person that I am
And that's all I want to be. Myself.

Chapter 13

Taking the Challenge

I've always enjoyed working with children and being around them. In 1987 I was reading the local newspaper *The Evening Post* when I saw a job advert for a playworker for two mornings a week at Purley Prep School. I applied for the role and attended an interview. I was happy when I got the job and was excited for the opportunity. It was great to meet my co-workers, meet the kids to read to them and play, it was fun. I really enjoyed it but over time the number of kids started to dwindle and the job came to an end in 1991.

I had now reached a time in my life where I was becoming more confident and I wanted to improve my life and future prospects. On one particular Tuesday in 1988 I enrolled at Wilson Adult Education College to study a basic English course. I never had a chance to complete my education in Barbados as a young girl so I felt I needed to get some qualifications to improve my standard of life. Also I knew at some stage that I would need to look for paid work now the kids were growing up. Every Tuesday morning from 10.00am til 12.00pm I would take my youngest daughter Louise to primary school then walk across the courtyard to attend lessons. I learnt how to compose sentences, grammar, spelling, words to use and how to communicate. I was a bit shy at first to go in to the class because I felt a bit silly to be a forty-four-year-old woman learning something so basic. I even met people from different backgrounds, such as one man from the Philippines, so it was an eye-opener to know I wasn't alone when it came to learning. I was surprised to know that people born in England were attending the class because I thought they had more education opportunities than myself who was born in the West Indies. I found the lessons interesting and I learnt a lot doing the homework – it even gave me confidence when being around people. I believe that education creates understanding and doing this course certainly gave me the knowledge I needed. I took the exam for GCSE English and I passed and received the qualification in November 1998 – I was over the moon and felt a great sense of achievement.

The kids were also progressing in their life. Colleen was doing well in her work as a travel agent, Nigel was enjoying a career as a car mechanic and soon made the move to work with a telecoms company. After Rodney left school he worked at Marks & Spencer part-time. Esther was studying and wanted to go on to further education and Jocelyn was studying to be a beauty therapist and working at the Body Shop and would go on to work at Marks & Spencer. The kids were working hard and making me proud. Things weren't easy and sometimes we would squabble, fight and not see eye to eye but that's what life can be like with different personalities. We still cared for each other and would try to support each other as much as possible. After all we were family and only had each other.

Life for me continued in a normal fashion, working part-time at Purley Prep School Monday and Thursday mornings while attending adult education college classes – juggling all this plus raising a growing family.

The time came as the children started to get older and started to pursue further education. My second youngest son told me that he wanted to continue his education by going to university. This was a shock because I didn't know anyone who had been to university before, no one in my family had been educated at a university level before but I always vowed that I would do my best in John's memory. Financially it was going to be tough because I was living on a widow's pension from the government and part-time wages. We were also fortunate to receive funding from our council local authority and Rodney received a grant for his studies.

So Rodney successfully applied for a place to enrol at Thames Polytechnic in London to study as an electronic engineer. Rodney was the first child to move away from home and live somewhere else – he would sometimes come back to Reading to visit or I would send him money to make sure he was surviving the student life.

I can remember while Rodney was studying in London, that he came home once to visit the family and he looked well but his clothes were shabby with holes. As a student, he couldn't afford to buy a new jumper because he was living on a tight budget. When he returned to London, I went to the Post

Office on a Tuesday – the day when I would receive my widow's pension from the government and I went to Marks & Spencer to buy a new jumper for him. I wrapped the item in brown paper and posted it to Rodney in London, it cost about £10.

As Rodney was about to finished his studies, my fourth child Esther decided that she also wanted to continue her studies. Esther enrolled at Greenwich University, again thankfully with the help of a government grant to finance her studies. These days were a testing time for me because I wanted to help my kids financially and it was tough but I was determined that I was going to give them the best that I could afford.

I will always remember the day of my Esther's graduation – it was a November morning in 1994. I got dressed that morning in a smart outfit and attended the event alongside Rodney and Esther as we drove to Westminster City Hall – I was one of the proudest mums on that day. Colleen had warned me I should take some tissues because I would shed some tears. I was so excited as I sat in the hall and heard my daughter's name and then saw Esther walk on to the rostrum as she received her certificate for business administration. I cried tears of joy and excitement and it was such a privileged opportunity that I never thought I would see.

The day to day routine of life continued. I would take Louise to school, prepare dinners, do the grocery shopping, do the washing and ironing. As the months rolled on, as a family we would celebrate birthdays, go out for meals for special occasions, go to work, celebrate new jobs and commiserate when things weren't going to plan – this was family life for the Chandlers. Life as I knew it was about to change again!

15th April 1990 would have been John's 49th birthday. It was also Easter Sunday and on this morning I went to church. It felt like a normal day but it would prove to be a day that would change my life. I was attending the West Reading Methodist Church on the Oxford Road and I had befriended members of the congregation such as David Geary. On this Sunday I was conducting praise of adoration which takes place at the start of service. David came to me at the end of the service and was praising me for doing a good job and he said, "Una – why don't you become a local preacher?" I was shocked and left the church quickly because it wasn't something that I had planned and I didn't take the suggestion seriously. On the following day, I was lying in my bed thinking about David's words, trying to make sense of his suggestions. I heard a voice come to me saying that I should read Exodus chapter 4, verse 2 of the Bible. In the passage God is speaking to Moses to convince him to go to the Israelites and it says, 'the voice of the lord says, what is that in your hand and Moses says a rod'. So when I read these few words, I felt that was the confirmation I needed to undertake the challenge to be a local preacher. I felt that God was using the Bible as a rod to reveal his message to me and I couldn't ignore the sign. I said to myself, "Lord I have got to do your will." The next day I went to see a few friends from church – Terry and Joyce Gibbs, Gordon Wilson and Madge to tell them about my plans. My dear friends cried with excitement and we prayed together about this new path and journey in my life.

Terry called Reverend John Stephens who was the superintendent minister of the church. All of a sudden I felt an urge that David was right and I had the gut feeling that I should undertake the challenge and start the training. John came to see me at my home a few days later to discuss the idea with me and if it was the right thing for me to do. As John was about to leave my home, he gave me some helpful advice – he said, "Una, always remember: do not try to copy other people or other preachers. Always be yourself." Even today I remember those words and they have stuck with me. John explained to me that I would have to study theology and have a mentor to help my studies. The studies would take just over three years and during the studies I would learn more about the Bible, how to conduct a service, writing sermons and having the confidence to preach before congregation.

I didn't have to go to college to do the studies, instead I was given a tutor called Dudley Coates but he became preoccupied with his day job so Elizabeth Carter became my tutor. I could go to Elizabeth's home in Caversham during the day about three times a month to learn and discuss the course in order to prepare for assignments, be given grades and receive feedback. My life was busy – juggling a part-time job, maintaining my studies and looking after my family and a home. As a single mother I had to juggle housework and studies with cooking and attending to the kids. I would often go and sit in the front room area of the house to get some peace and quiet away from the TV and noise so I could focus and concentrate. Over the three-year course, I was given thirty assignments to cover theology as a subject. I had to learn about a new style of worship, how to write prayers, how to run a service for kids and how to choose hymns to coincide with themes of sermons. I enjoyed learning about the topic in detail – this was an opportunity for me to gain a wider understanding of religion and faith.

I was also given a supervising mentor called John Coleman who was also a local preacher. I could go to John and talk about any concerns I had with my studies and he would give me practical lessons on how to write prayers and sermons, guiding me through the early days.

When I was working on the assignments, I found it tough. All I knew about theology was growing up in church in Barbados and reading the Bible – studying religion as a topic was something new and I wasn't used to it.

I had grown up attending a Pentecostal Church with a style of worship that was vibrant, with lots of gospel singing, shouting and clapping hands. Basically praising God with all of your strength and energy. In the Methodist Church, the style of worship is calmer, more reserved and a lot more orderly and organised. It was a new way of worshipping and I had to learn how to conduct services in this new fashion. I knew I had to adapt, it was intimidating but I knew I could do it.

Over time, through my studies I learnt that praising God sincerely could be done in different ways – you didn't have to make a lot of noise to engage with God and have a spiritual faith. The real challenges came when I had to take exams and I failed the first one – I didn't feel prepared for the first one and I found it daunting. If I didn't pass the exam – I wouldn't be able to gain the qualification. The tutors were concerned that I wouldn't be able to pass the exam because I had stopped attending school when I was thirteen years old – some felt that my level of education wasn't good enough to pass the exam. At one stage, it looked like all of my efforts and hard work would be in vain and I wouldn't be able to complete the course and become a local preacher. Tom Stuckey was the replacement superintendent after John Stephens and when he heard about my struggles with the exams he gave me a lot of support and even offered to give me a passing grade because he believed in me. He knew that I had the ability and the knowledge but I simply found it difficult to demonstrate this knowledge in exams in order to get a passing grade.

I didn't want any pity or an easy ticket and I wanted to prove that I could do it by myself – all I needed was time to revise the topics and resit the exam. If I was going to qualify as a local preacher – I had to pass the exam. I was determined to succeed. Looking back on these tough times – I remember the support and love of my family and friends who gave me lots of encouragement. Even though I was struggling, I never had any doubt and I knew that being a local preacher was the right thing to do.

The second time around I felt more prepared and I resat the exam and I passed it. I felt ecstatic to know that I had conquered a great challenge and I could now qualify as a local preacher. In February 1995 I was accredited and I was given an official church service to acknowledge that I was qualified to be a local preacher. The service was held at the West Reading Methodist Church on a Sunday evening with 150 people in the congregation to help me celebrate passing this milestone.

This was a busy period in my life. As Rodney and Esther finished their further education – then came the challenge to learn to drive.

I always think that learning to drive is a life skill that is handy to have so one by the one the kids asked me for my help in learning to drive. Nigel and Colleen had learnt to drive while John was alive so now it was the rest of the kids who wanted to learn. I would make sure that the kids had registered with a driving instructor who could teach them the dos and don'ts of driving. To give them extra practice we would go out driving using my car – I would drive to a quiet area like an industrial estate on Portman Road and let them at different times (Esther, Rodney or Jocelyn) practice straight driving and manoeuvres. Sometimes we look back at those days with laughter remembering times spent driving together and preparing for them to pass their driving test.

Never Give Up

I'll fight to the end although the way may be tough
I'll never give up though the way may seem rough
I'll reach to the end of life problems some day
I'll fight to the end and will never give up.

Chapter 14

Being More Confident

I never knew the real me and my true ability until I was put under pressure. I always saw myself as a mother who loved cooking, baking, cleaning and doing all of the household chores and that was all I knew and all I did. Until one night I lay in bed thinking and I reached for a pen and paper that I kept by my bedside.

Out of the blue I began writing some words which formed poems. 'Do Not Wait Until Tomorrow' was my first poem. 'Take Each Day With a Prayer' was the second poem. 'Smile and be Happy' was the third poem and the work continued. I wrote another called 'What is Life' where I began to question the challenges of life.

These words were simply what came to mind and what I felt at the time. When I finished writing I looked at the page and I was shocked and surprised to see that I had written a whole poem. I didn't even know I had the ability to do it but I was pleased that I could do something special and there was something more to come. The next day I showed the piece of work to my youngest daughter to see her reaction and she was amazed at the words she read and said, "Oh my god Mum – you've written a poem." I didn't even realise that was what it was – my life was beginning to change.

I found that my poems could express the feelings and thoughts within me while I lived my life from day to day. Writing the poems gave me a joy and peace to know that I was achieving something special on paper.

Over time I began submitting more poems to my church magazine plus I would write articles on various subjects about my life working for the nursery school and sermons that had an impact on me.

I have always been a keen reader of magazines and newspapers and I noticed adverts for poetry competitions and writers could submit their work.

I got a real buzz for doing more and more poetry work so I soon joined local and national poetry groups to enter my work for poetry competitions, which gave me the opportunity of having my work published into poetry collections that would be sold across the UK.

I attended poetry reading classes in my local town once a month with my son so I could share my work with other local writers. Every few weeks we would meet in a venue on Silver Street to read poems to each other and give each other praise and feedback – it was great to applaud each other's efforts. These sessions helped me with my confidence to share my work and it validated that I had something valuable to say.

Over the years I was lucky enough to have my work showcased in different books and I shared my poems with various people. I felt that I wanted to publish my poems and create a book that included just my work. In 2006 I worked with a publisher to create my poetry book and I called it *Rainbow*. The reason for this title was because I felt that I had a real struggle raising a young family as a single parent but I always believed that things would get better and improve and I would find my rainbow.

I had twenty-five books printed and I gave them to friends and family members to say 'thank you' for the support they had shown me in difficult times of my life over the years.

Life was changing at a fast pace and running a house was a costly expense. Any money I had saved was being used for food, bills, clothes and maintaining a home and making ends meet was tough. After John's death I received some money from Gillette (the company where John worked) which kept me and the family going and helped me to pay the bills.

I always loved working with kids and I had plenty of experience working as a nursery nurse. I applied for a job working at Thameside Primary School in 1996-1997 as a dinner lady. It was a bit difficult and I didn't enjoy it.

At this time I felt I wanted to give something back to the community and keep myself busy because I like to be active so I applied to a local Age Concern charity shop that needed voluntary workers. In 1997, I went along for an interview and got the role working in the shop on Thursday mornings 9.00am – 1.00pm. I enjoyed helping the customers when they came in to the shop looking sad, lonely and helpless then kitting them out with new clothes and items. I would help them find the best fitting garments for them to wear and send them home looking their best. I still have the memories of those times. I made friends and learnt about serving customers and working in a shop so I enjoyed it.

I then decided I would look for a job working with children – one weekday afternoon I walked into the entrance of my local Asda supermarket and I saw a job advert on the notice board for the English Martyrs Catholic School who were looking for a playworker for an evening afterschool club. I did the application, had an interview and got the job in 1998.

Life was going great. The kids were working and progressing in life – having moved out in to their own properties. Suddenly I got the news in July 1998 that my father had passed away at the age of seventy-nine. My dad had been sick in the latter years of his life so in a way I wasn't surprised. I booked a flight to Barbados and flew to the island with my sons Rodney and Nigel. It was a sad occasion but I was glad I was there and I saw relatives that I hadn't seen in years.

I returned to work then I started at a new school in 1999 – Wilson Afterschool Club which was nice because my kids attended this school and it brought back fond memories. Plus it was closer to home so I could simply walk from my house and it was less than ten minutes away. I received training that gave me the skills and qualifications to be a playworker. In the meantime I continued working in the charity shop because I found it to be very rewarding and I worked there until 2001. I was carving out a career for myself and it felt great.

My Kind of People

So often while out and about on my travels
There are many people who I sometimes meet
Like the beggar man along the wayside
Or the travelling person who has lost their way
My kind of people with just a house to call home
Not a cottage, a palace or a great mansion
Just a comfortable home neatly furnished
The kind of people who will always welcome me.
The kind of people who will face each day
Fearing the postman's knock on the door
Or perhaps going to that bargain shop
Seeking how to save one pence or two
Those were the kind of people that I did love best
As I used to serve them up something special
With that look in their eyes would often say
'Thank you'
For those were the kind of people
That I would so often meet.

Chapter 15

A Committed Life

My life had changed so much. Not only was I now a Methodist lay preacher fully accredited in February 1995 but I still felt the urge that there was still more spiritual work for me to do.

One day, while attending my local church on a Sunday evening in October 2000, I saw an advert in the church magazine. The advert was describing a vacancy for a chaplain and I had never heard of a chaplain but it sounded different. I discovered that a chaplain is a person who supports employees in the workplace at Reading Borough Council.

I mulled the idea over and I didn't understand the responsibility of the role but I knew I wanted to find out more.

I rang a phone number that was given with the job advert to enquire about the role. A gentleman called John Frew answered the phone and we had a brief chat – John agreed to come and meet me in my home to discuss the role of a volunteer chaplain. When we met, I was able to ask questions – I discovered that I would be dealing with people on a regular one to one basis. I would be meeting people from various cultures and backgrounds to listen to their personal or workplace issues and concerns and give them support. During the discussion I became excited and it was something different from everyday life looking after a home and doing chores. I liked the idea of being out and about to meet people to give me a new outlook on life. I felt this was a different adventure and way to use my faith. Before John left, we prayed about the new role for my life.

After meeting with me, John felt I was the right person for the role so he spoke to Superintendent Jim Booth (senior minister of the Methodist Church for the Reading area) and recommended that he had found the right person for the job and the search for a new chaplain to Reading Borough Council was over.

John then passed my details to Sue Penson – the lady who would assign me to the role and help to train me up. I was set to replace the current retiring chaplain Frank Morris so I would have to learn the ropes from him. I met with Sue on a few occasions to go in to detail about the role and, during the second meeting, Sue booked a meeting with a senior representative from the Reading Borough Council to receive his approval for my appointment to the role. This was the first time that I had entered a building in Reading town centre called Fountain House. I enjoyed being in this professional and business-like environment and I felt like I was in my element – it was exciting and I never thought I would be visiting offices like this, I had never expected this to happen to me. The view from floor seven of Fountain House was amazing because I could see the whole of Broad Street and I was in awe as I drank coffee and talked about the exciting challenges ahead of me. I was briefed by Reading Borough Council about the role, my conduct and the areas of the building that I could access to provide pastoral support to the staff. The most important thing that I remember about this meeting was the importance of confidentiality when speaking to staff members. I was told that I would be successfully accepted in to the role and I was authorised to receive an official Reading Borough Council pass to access different parts of the building.

At the time I was a bit daunted about the things I would have to learn and all the new faces and people I would meet so I agreed to take the role on a trial basis for three months to see if the role suited me and if I would be successful.

The responsibility of the role started to dawn on me. There would be a lot to learn so I met my predecessor Frank Morris for coffee one day at St Mary's Church so we could share ideas. I looked Frank in the eye and asked the simple question, "Tell me how you felt walking in to the building on your first day?" I asked the question because the role of the chaplain is representing God and your faith so how will people accept you in this role – whether they have a faith or not. I suppose I wanted the confirmation from Frank of his experience and how he felt. Frank told me that at the time he felt like he was thrown in to a lion's den. This was his way of explaining how daunting the task can be. My reaction and feeling was – I'll have a go and try it for myself.

The next step was to visit the council offices on two occasions with Frank to see him in action and to be shown around the building and learn the ropes for the role. I felt a bit timid and a bit lost. The building is large and has fifteen floors with lots of people doing their daily work, phones ringing and people tapping on keyboards at computers. It was strange to be in these surroundings because it was unfamiliar. I was used to being in a church with a congregation who wanted to hear about Christianity and faith.

Now I was in office surroundings with new people and I would need to strike up the confidence to talk to strangers and introduce myself and my role. Most people I would be meeting would not have a religious faith and would not have heard about the role of a chaplain so I was new to them and they were new to me. I also had to find a way to break the ice with people and find a way of talking to them without an agenda of faith. Also I had to remember that these people had work to do so I didn't want to be a distraction or get in the way.

I soon began to realise I would have to share my life experience with strangers and perhaps people that I never knew before.

I decided that Wednesday would be the day to perform the chaplain role so I could get in to a routine and so the staff could get used to seeing me in the building.

The day came very quickly for me to enter the building by myself without Frank. That morning I prayed and asked God for courage and strength to face the challenge. In those early days I remember two people in particular who took the time to talk to me and make me feel comfortable – Annette Paterson and Michael Holt. Having a few familiar faces that I recognised was helpful and made me feel at ease being in strange surroundings.

I got to the building and I met the security staff at

the entrance and I greeted them with, "Good Morning." I met with Michael Holt, a section leader, and he took me to meet a team of his staff. For the next hour I chatted to the team of fifteen people, we shook hands and had a quick chit chat and the day was over.

The second time I went to the RBC offices by myself, I met with Annette on level six of the building and I introduced myself to her to make her acquaintance. We had a nice chat about my role and about her job – Annette was a manager and she took me around the whole building to show me around and introduce me to people (especially managers). For the next few hours I would learn a lot, see new faces and I felt honoured that someone recognised my purpose of being at the offices. I felt like I had made a real breakthrough from being a shy person who was afraid to approach people to having the confidence to find my way around a vast building. To this day, I still feel like I owe Annette and Michael a great deal of gratitude for their help and support.

After the first two occasions of visiting the council offices by myself, I felt empowered to take on the challenge of being a chaplain – when I walked in to the office, people recognised me and soon strangers became acquaintances and friendly faces. The weeks passed by really quickly and the three months came and went so fast that I didn't realise. I was happy to do the role. I was soon given a name badge that would break the ice for me – it was a symbol that I was in the building on official business in an official role and not a random person wandering around.

As I became familiar with the staff members we would talk about family issues, relatives who were ill, children, shopping, matrimonial problems, hobbies and any concerns that they had in the workplace. I always made sure that I listened and I cared about their situation with empathy. If the topic of conversation was confidential, I would take their contact number to have a private chat with them and offer some support and advice. As the weeks, months and years continued my confidence and familiarity with RBC and the staff grew.

As time continued, I was honoured with some great achievements. I was interviewed in 2002 by a gentleman called Victor Sylvester for a magazine called *Flame* that talks about the Methodist Church. Victor asked me about my work and he took my photograph while I stood outside of the Reading Borough Council office and I felt proud to think that my work was being acknowledged.

In 2004 I was asked to write about my Christian journey and chaplaincy work for a book called *Day In, Day Out* and I was pleased to be involved. Then in 2007, as part of my chaplaincy role to Reading Borough Council, I experienced an exciting moment and received surprising news. I was nominated for a customer service award for being kind, helpful and thoughtful. I don't know who nominated me because it was a secret. I received a certificate and it was a nice way to be acknowledged and thanked for my work.

April 2001 saw the start of my chaplaincy journey and I'm proud to say that I have continued my voluntary role. I feel like it is a role that has been fulfilling, I have greeted new staff members as they joined the organisation, I have wished some people well as they have left to get a new job or retire. I have consoled people during grief and stressful times such as job cuts and changes. I have conducted memorial services for staff members who have passed away.

Often I have been asked why I chose to be a chaplain – volunteering my time and efforts for free. My main motivation has been a way for me to say thank you and give something back to the community. During John's illness, he was given good care and support and I felt that being a chaplain would be worthwhile.

Over the years I have shared my stories and experiences with the people I have met. I am never too afraid to share with people a little about my past experiences because it helps many folks to understand that many of us face the same challenges and problems in our lives and that they are not alone.

April 2011 was a significant time because it marked ten years of being a chaplain. A ceremony organised by RBC, my mentor Susan Van Beveren and my family took place at the council offices to acknowledge my voluntary role and the contribution. I made a speech to thank those who attended and supported me for the ten years. Reflecting on the ten years, I see the staff as a key part of me delivering the chaplaincy role because they have shown me kindness and respect to allow me the opportunity to address their pastoral needs.

I can certainly say that the role is rewarding, doing something I love and being around people. I think the chaplaincy role brings out the real me –

someone who is nurturing, patient and thoughtful. I realise that the skills I learnt during my lay preacher training have come in useful for my chaplaincy. It gives me the diplomacy, and understanding of people and ways to conduct myself in different surroundings.

I'm now fifteen years in to the chaplaincy journey and to this day, I meet a lot of employees who have never heard of a chaplain and they are unsure of what the role is about. I take pride to explain to them that I am there to support the employees of RBC and be alongside them and give support as a confidential listening ear when I can. Being a chaplain makes me proud to be who I am. Even as I continue in the role as chaplain, I never take anything or anyone for granted – I always say thank you to the staff for sharing their time with me.

I have come a long way from the seventeen-year-old girl who arrived in England with a suitcase, far away from Barbados.

Looking back – my upbringing in Barbados made me the person I am and has done me the world of good. Watching my dear mother scrimp and save, wash and wear, make ends meet and serve up small meals I knew that life could be hard but it doesn't always have to stay that way.

My life has changed from being a sad, lonely widow and raising a family. The kids have grown up and now they follow their own path in life, getting jobs and gaining successful careers.

Now they're grown up I look back and remember times when the kids needed new school shoes and I didn't have enough money – I would pop to the cobblers to see Alex Kellyway who was kind enough to mend the shoes for cheap. It may not seem a lot but often it made the difference as an essential way of life. Alex was a great source of support to me – a friendly ear to listen to my moans and groans and a smile to cheer me up.

Even during challenging times my faith in God remained strong – sometimes I would turn my head and look to heaven and say to God, "Stop the world and just let me step off," because that was how I often felt.

But now, not only am I a mother but I have made plenty of friends from my preaching around the Methodist circuit and they show me the greatest love and respect.

Ultimately I'm grateful to God that my children are in good health and peace of mind.

Only Human

I am only human, that I must not forget
I've got my moments when like others I sometimes
forget
Fed up and tired, lonely and feeling sad
For human I am and I must not forget
The bills, the car and the house in need of repair
I am in despair for I am only a human
The pain and the hurt cannot be seen
When deep within me I am only human
I look around me I see worse conditions
With difficulties trouble and sorrow
The problems are with me the longer that I live
It is only when I die that my problems will die too
All of my heart, soul, and mind I am a human
The need to do better each day I will hope
For all through my life I must not forget
Human I am and human I will always be.

Chapter 16

My Future

Often in life, opportunities occur when you're not expecting it and you can find yourself embarking on a journey.

As the family were steadily growing up and I had a few more pounds in my pocket, I would take my young daughters for daytrips on coaches to tourist attractions in London. It didn't happen a lot but it did give us a chance to get out and about to do something different and give the kids something to look forward to.

As the girls got older, they started to occupy themselves, get part-time jobs and they became busy with their studies in further education. At this stage, even though my family needed me, they were becoming a bit more self-sufficient and able to look after themselves so I decided it was time to have a bit more time for me.

My daughter Colleen would often buy me the women's lifestyle magazine *Bella*. I recall in 1998 reading one particular issue with various articles on health, fashion and food recipes when my eyes caught sight of adverts with offers on travel holidays and trips. I've always had a sense of adventure hidden inside of me and I had a desire for travelling. With coaching holidays, you would be collected at a particular location and driven to your holiday destination. I liked this idea because it meant I could visit different locations in an independent fashion while being safe.

I was curious to find out more about these trips so I called up the travel companies and began asking questions. I started to make notes of places around England that I had never seen before and I would call coach companies and request some holiday brochures. As the brochures came via the post, I got more and more curious about some of the places listed. In the past I had gone on a few daytrips with the kids or coaching holidays to seaside resorts with Louise because she was youngest. We had visited Cornwall, Eastbourne, Isle of Wight and Dorset.

Now Louise was grown up and a teenager she no longer wanted to accompany me on trips so I decided to travel on my own. Before I knew it, I had booked my first trip, it was to Exeter with an overnight stay and it was to celebrate Mother's Day.

I waited for the coach in Reading town centre and I felt excited yet a bit insecure and uncertain about the trip. It was rare for me to be away from home, from my familiar surroundings and the kids and for the next few days I would be by myself. It was a big step but I thought I would give it a go. When I booked the trip I was given the seat number '6' which would prove to be a bit of a lucky charm for me to meet my first travel friend. After the coach left Reading, it would stop off at different towns and locations to pick up other customers for the trip. The coach stopped in Newbury and a gracious elderly lady got on to the coach and sat next to me. Her name was Rachel Ham and we got on straight away. She was outgoing and chatty and from the time she sat next to me, we introduced ourselves, talking about our lives and the reasons why we travelled. I'll always remember Rachel because she gave me a lot of confidence and she made me realise that travelling around by yourself was nothing to fear. I was new to coach travelling so Rachel took me under her wing and tenderly looked after me on that first trip. I made an effort to buy a thank you card while on the trip and I gave it to her before we parted because I wanted to thank her for the kindness she had shown me. From that day we became good friends until she passed away in 2010.

As my family begun to get older and have their own lives – this gave me the freedom to go on more trips. Sometimes two or three times in a year I would go away to places like Falmouth, Norfolk, Blackpool twice, Isle of Wight, Glasgow, Llandudno, Newcastle. Liverpool, Stockport, Eastbourne, Bournemouth, Italy, Scotland, Newquay and Stafford upon Avon

I see travelling as an adventure – you see the nature and scenery, you meet different people from various places and when you strike up conversation you learn a lot. It's about experiencing life. If you stay in the house, you won't see or do anything so I always enjoy going out and about to have a break from the day to day routine.

As the months and years continued, I would buy postcards from the locations I visited as a visual reminder of the places I've seen.

It is true that travel broadens the mind and I

certainly agree because for over fifteen years this is how I have spent my spare time.

When I'm away on a trip and Sunday comes I will try to find a church to worship and attend a service. On one trip I went to the Holy Island in Northumberland as an excursion during Easter weekend. On the Holy Island there are two small churches, a post office and a community hall – a simple small place that is quaint and beautiful. While walking around I heard singing coming from a church so I walked in to the Anglican Church and sat down to enjoy the service – it was so serene and calm, it felt good to be there. On this particular trip the whole group was taken on a Catherine Cookson trail – we had the opportunity to learn about the author, her birthplace and the inspiration for her books. I learnt a lot from Catherine's life story because it taught me that you can start out in life with humble beginnings and aspire to great things.

The trip which will always be in my heart and memories was the trip to Italy in 2005. Even though I don't speak Italian, I was able to get along fine on the trip with the help of a designated tour guide. We visited the Vatican City and I saw famous artwork by Michelangelo and I was privileged to walk around the island of Capri. It was a trip of a lifetime because the country is such a beautiful place. Another trip that sticks in my memory was my trip to Edinburgh in 2006 – a place that I always wanted to visit for a long time. I enjoyed Edinburgh because of the statues and monuments, the castles and the famous Princes Street. I also had the chance to walk around the length and breadth of the Royal Yacht, Britannia that was docked. We were given hand-held audio devices that would give you directions and information as you were walking around the yacht.

I can still remember as I stepped in to the hallway of the ship I saw photographs of the royal family that the Queen had displayed. I suppose I was surprised because we put the Queen on a pedestal and I didn't expect to see personal photographs that she cherished. I often see these places on TV programmes and I say, "Oh I've been there," while chuckling to myself and recounting the memories.

Before I knew it, I had become a professional traveller – my family were concerned for my safety at first because I was travelling alone but it didn't take long for me to become settled and content. I am happy with my life, for me I cannot ask for more.

There are trips you plan and some you dread. I got a call in March 2007 to say my mother was sick and the family needed me to go back to the island. I flew to the island by myself and spent a few weeks with my mum while she was silent in bed and I comforted her in her final days. She passed away just before I was due to come back to England so I stayed to help prepare for the funeral. Colleen flew over to the island to attend the funeral as we said goodbye to my mum. The trip was a sad occasion but it was good to go back to my mother country.

Travelling came at the right time in my life – it helped me to continue moving on with my grief and start a new chapter.

Over the years I have made some great friends and met people from all over the country – lovely genuine people and we still keep in touch and write to each other to keep the friendships going. Through travelling I have been able to build a new life for myself and it takes courage and some bravery to be a single traveller but now I do it, there's no looking back for me now.

Keep Travelling On

I have travelled by car and on the bus
I have travelled by air and also on sea
I have travelled places, only by chance
But deep inside my heart I have always missed
home.
I have travelled on land very near to home
Where all around me I see people.
I have travelled to the shop, the park and school
Where I sometimes meet friends that I know.
As each day comes we go travelling
When the night draws in, we must rest.
We wait and dream for another new day
When once again we go travelling, travelling on.

Chapter 17

How Times have Changed

I often look at life as trying to climb a mountain – you stand at the bottom and try to understand how to climb and progress in life but as time goes on, things get a bit easier.

Just when I thought that it would be time to sit back and have a rest – my youngest daughter Louise would grow up and also request to learn to drive by following the footsteps of her brothers and sisters. Louise attended Winchester University in Hampshire in 2001 and graduated in 2004 then extended her studies for an extra year to earn a MA at Farnborough College.

This was an exciting time as Louise graduated at Winchester Cathedral for her first degree then I was privileged to attend another graduation at the Guildford Cathedral as Louise was presented with her certificate for all of her studies. I have learnt that through life there are challenges and there is no such a thing as a prefect family. Like so many families we had our share of ups and downs like a rollercoaster ride but we stuck together.

I have also learnt that life moves on quickly. My greatest joy was to learn that I was to become a grandmother. My eldest son Nigel and his partner Susan had Jordan in June 1994. In December 2000, my daughter Colleen had Ciara and in 2004 Samuel was born to my son Rodney and his partner Mary with Josie being born in 2008.

I am still watching my family and thinking to myself how on earth did I manage to do it? With the running of a home and making sure that everyone was fed, healthy and looking their best. I certainly feel like I've come a long way and achieved a great deal to raise a family by myself and continue John's legacy now he is not with us.

My life has changed in many ways – I am now in my late sixties, approaching my seventieth birthday and life experiences have made me a lot wiser. I realised that when a loved one dies your world will still go on and that the world has not stopped.

I learnt that when we have our loved ones, we can take our life for granted and things can change very quickly.

I did make one promise after the death of my husband John – that I would always keep the family home. It was a place that held many memories and was the main place for the family to meet for meals, family occasions and Christmas.

As the years continued, the children grew up, saved money and decided they wanted to buy homes of their own. One by one, Nigel, Colleen, Rodney, Jocelyn and Esther bought their own homes in the Reading area. Some of the kids would move out to rent a property then come back to the family home to save enough money for a deposit for a mortgage. Elm Lodge Avenue was the place that we could all call home in one way or another. As time continued the house needed more DIY, decorating and expensive repair work like a new roof, a new kitchen and boiler. With the kids all moved out (Louise was at university studying), being in the big family home by myself seemed silly when I was the only one living there. The house needed a lot of expensive maintenance work and as the years came and went quickly I noticed that the area around me was changing and not for the better. The small close-knit community where everyone knew each other, local amenities and a safe neighbourhood had gone. When we moved to the West Reading Oxford Road area in 1973 it was a thriving community with a butcher's, bank, newsagent, cobblers, familiar neighbours who were friendly – all the things you needed to raise a family. In 2001, the area looked remarkably different and it didn't feel like home anymore. Suddenly, one day I woke up and decided that I would put the family home up for sale and move. Moving house is known as being stressful and hard work but I felt that the time was right for me to put the house up for sale.

I gathered the family around me and told them my decision. The kids had grown up in the house and saw it as the family home where they had a lot of happy memories. The thought of selling up and leaving was too much to bear and the kids were upset that Elm Lodge Avenue would no longer be known as the family home. I remember the 'for sale' sign was put outside of the house and Rodney would take the sign down because he didn't want me to move. I spoke to him and explained my reasons for selling – my mind was made up and in time he would agree it was for the best even though it was emotionally hard to let go of a house that had so many fond memories for our family.

After almost thirty years – we would be moving.

I never thought I would have the strength to move – it is very stressful and challenging but without any regrets or sadness, the house transaction was completed and I packed the boxes. Over the coming months I packed up the front room with the ornaments and books where we would entertain guests. I packed away the kitchen items, packed away the bedroom items and prepared to leave.

On 28th March 2002, we packed up our belongings and said goodbye to the family home and left. We hired a removal van which arrived to load up large items of furniture. I can still remember the last few moments as I locked the front door for the final time. The kids were very upset and tearful but I felt fine – it felt like the right time to move, a new beginning and a fresh start with no regrets. The loss of my husband will always stay with me and I learnt the hard way – life is for living. I often say to friends and my family that when bad things happen in life, we can't turn the clock back so we should try to move on.

I am happy with my life and I cannot ask for more. Anything I have achieved comes from having wisdom, knowledge and learning to cope even in my darkest times.

Sometimes people ask me, "How did you cope as a young widow?" My response: "I had no choice – I had to get on with life. I felt like I was thrown in to the deep and dark waters of life and I had to sink or swim. I chose to swim along and get through the choppy waters until things were calmer."

For me, life is good. I sometimes look back and reminiscence and of course I am only human. So I wonder what my life would have been like if my husband was here. I am grateful for my children and my lovely, beautiful grandchildren who bring me great joy and happiness.

I am thankful to God for all of his protection, his love and his care over myself and my family. I look back and reminisce with contentment and peace.

Moving On

How the times have changed since we were born
With fast cars, computers click, click, they will go
With messages going quick and fast
Keeping up with the times it is all so true
With the fast food and the take-away shops
It's all happening, look how far we have come
In those days we were told we must try a little
harder
The harder we try we are losing the battle
For moving with the times there are lessons to be
learnt.

Chapter 18

Exciting Times

My family excites me and bringing them up as a single parent was very stressful but I am proud of them and always will be. I'm not just a mum, I was also my children's guardian, I am a friend – a shoulder to cry on, a confidante, a listening ear and someone to protect them. I am not only a mum, but I'm also a dad. I am there to celebrate when times are going good, when the kids pass exams or get a new job and have exciting news. But also there to commiserate when there are sad times and disappointments. Throughout the years we have worked as a team to get to where we are today. I may be the head of the family but as a family we have supported each other. The older kids helped out with the younger ones and I couldn't be prouder.

We've only ever had each other to rely on and we've stuck together like glue. In John's lifetime the children were always close to him and he was a really good father. As parents John and I assumed a role – I would mostly do the wifely duties such as household chores and John would take the kids shopping, walking and even chase them around for fun. Often when we were in church he would take them for a walk along the river and treat them to an ice cream or a sweet treat. Sweets for him were a treat because his face would always beam when he saw the kids happy. He was a firm father and if one of the kids was naughty, he would speak firmly and with authority like a father with knowledge and wisdom. He was a real family man.

Since John passed I have been their confidante and on various occasions have given them words of encouragement – "Cheer up, things will get better." For me I always had one thought in my mind, one of these days life will somehow get better.

John was a real family man and proud of his children, sometimes I have visions of him enjoying the benefits of his grandchildren – playing with them, taking them to buy sweets and spoiling them.

If John had lived to enjoy the grandchildren, he would have made a fuss of them. So now without him, it's my turn. They are like the icing on the cake and they do make me laugh. I look forward to seeing the grandkids grow up and I cherish every moment of my time with them.

Sadly, he has missed out on so much. It is now the grandchildren that keep me going because I like making a fuss of them.

I see a lot of traits of John in the grandkids – their love of life and how they enjoy singing. They are also very talkative and I can see so much of him in them. I tell myself that my husband is still around for me. I can see that the grandkids are his legacy.

I often take some time for myself as I look back and see how far I have been with my life mentally, physically and spiritually.

My work in the community has continued even

more. In 2012 I was given the opportunity to represent Reading Borough Council at regular citizenship ceremonies. For some people, it is a real achievement to become a British citizen so a significant event takes place to celebrate the occasion in a meaningful way. At the ceremony, individuals or large groups of people are welcomed into the local community and they get to meet other people in the area who are becoming British citizens.

When I'm at the ceremony, speeches will be made including some words spoken by myself where I encourage the new citizens to play an active role within their communities. The new people make an oath of allegiance and they take a pledge – I shake hands with people, give a speech and take lots of photographs with the excited people who are happy with their new status as British citizens. I find it exciting that I am involved in these ceremonies because I get to meet new people and it's an honour to think that I am involved in their life, in such a significant way. Often, the new citizens thank me and the other officials for the input in to the ceremony and they are grateful for the words that I said and the well wishes. It's also nice to know that the skills and talents that I possess can be used in a positive way.

Now, my life has changed and the kids even look after me. Sometimes we go out for meals, meet for coffee and go on outings to garden centres, theatre or fun places and it's nice.

I've always enjoyed cooking and baking from a young age as a girl growing up in Barbados and in these latter years, I find myself baking West Indian coconut bread (cake) more often. Some things never change. I get excited watching the family eating and having fun when we have chatty, lively get-togethers.

At times I still cannot believe that I am the woman who has come this far. From doing household chores in Barbados, working in a factory, cleaning offices and doing a variety of jobs to the person I am today.

I often think that God has a reason for what he has done.

What About Now

Of all the things that I'd like to be
I'd like to be myself
Laughing, crying, playing and cooking
Having fun-time most of all
I am not special as I often say
I am a mother and a grandmother
With brothers, sisters and cousins also
Which make me proud to be myself
I cannot pretend to be someone else
What good will it be when I am only me
With all of the fuss of being a mother
This makes me proud to be who I am.

Chapter 19

My Journey through Life

Nothing could have prepared me for this journey through life. For me personally this was a journey with many experiences. For me life is like a rollercoaster ride as I look ahead to each day wondering what challenges lie ahead.

The words of the old negro song stayed within me: 'nobody knows the trouble I've seen, nobody knows but Jesus'. It was these words which kept me going even when I felt like I was falling in to despair. Looking back I often wonder how did I manage?

I always remember sometimes when the weather was bad I would lie in bed and listen to the wind and rain howling outside of the window. The next morning after I took Louise to school I would often walk along Richmond Road (the street that ran parallel with my road) and I would look at the roof of my home to check it was still in one piece, making sure that slates were not missing and that my home was ok. My house was the only thing I had left and being a single mum – I dreaded having to do major repairs to the house that would be expensive.

This was a journey of tears, joy, fun, laughter and also sadness. Sadness for my children who had to grow up without a father. Sadness because I was left as a widow at the age of thirty-eight. Looking back on the early days of losing my husband – I would lie in bed and constantly think of the night John left me. During his lifetime he would say that he wouldn't live to reach the age of fifty but I never believed it. As I felt the pain of my loss, I let out one large scream as I struggled to come to terms with life without him. It simply seemed impossible that he wasn't around.

As the months rolled by, I would be at home with the baby (Louise) and I began to feel the pain of my loss. I would try and distract myself to keep busy but often there was nothing I could do to stop myself missing him. I called out my name and asked myself, "Una? Is it really me? Is it really me that has lost my husband?" The shock was terrible.

This was a journey of raising my kids. Watching the children grow in to teenagers and turn in to adults – men and women. All of my sacrifices and struggles were worthwhile. With John gone, life had to continue as the kids continued their education, found jobs, aspired to great careers and built a life of their own. I am so proud of how far we have come.

One of my purposes in life come what may is to hold on to my faith and trust in my God as a constant in my life that gives me strength and courage. As a Christian I always loved singing gospel songs and listening to other artists. I will always cherish the words of a song written and sang by an American artist called Andrae Crouch. The song is called 'Through it All' and it gave me the strength to be strong as I kept on smiling through my pain.

John was a popular man with many friends but I

witnessed how things can change. When life is on the up, there are plenty of friends to smile and enjoy the good times. But when life gets tough – some friends cannot always be found to be loyal and supportive. In the early days after John passed I needed the support, a friendly shoulder to cry on. But I could not find these friends. It seemed that as I walked along the lonely streets, the same friends saw me and ignored me. Immune to my grief. Maybe they didn't know what to say. I suppose there's only so many times that someone can say 'sorry to hear you lost your husband'. I only had my kids and we had to stick together and muddle through the challenges. As time continued, a few people would pop in to the family home to keep me company but I reflect back on my dark times and recall a sense of loneliness.

In my mind I always imagined my life as a rainbow high up in the sky. With its spectrum of colours – it represents hope and faith that things will improve and get better.

I reflect back on the challenging times and remember certain songs. In my early days of grief especially on Saturday afternoons I would sit and watch television with musicians singing music. Around 1985 a singer called Mick Hucknall sang 'Holding Back the Years'. I would sit and listen to that song willing Mick Hucknall to keep singing that song as I held my baby girl in my arms, rocking her to sleep.

Bill Withers sings a song called 'Lean on Me'. For me this song gave me comfort because I believed I could lean on God who was there for me in times of trouble.

Another song that meant a lot to me is Peter

Gabriel's song called 'Don't Give Up'. Whenever I heard it – I was determined to keep going against all odds. I do honestly believe that God allowed those songs to bring me comfort and solace.

My journey was an experience and a learning curve with plenty of hard work, commitment and dedication with love throughout.

It has made me stronger and wiser as an independent woman and brought many surprises.

One of the recent highlights of my life journey was in 2013 – being the mother of the bride to my daughter Jocelyn who married Matthew Hawkins on 2nd August. I had the honour of walking Jocelyn down the aisle to give her away. It would normally be a father's duty to perform this job but I had the privilege and it was great.

I always say life is what you make it – I have certainly learnt this and I wouldn't change a thing. I miss John everyday of my life but I am grateful to him for the time we had together. I am grateful for my six children and grandchildren – this my life.

My Youthful Days

When I was young I would skip along
I would often run as fast as I could
I would play games with others and have much fun
For youth is a time to be jolly and happy
Now as I get older with my everyday aches
I know it is my age telling me this
The pace of life seems slower
As I am moving slower and slower
I am not skipping along like I once did
My journey seems to be getting longer
Fun times – I must take more care
Alas I am beginning to feel my age
I have given up on those youthful days now
For those days I haven't forgotten
As the years and days swiftly go by
Each day now is enough for me.

Bajan Proverbs

As a young girl growing up in Barbados, I would often find myself surrounded by the 'old people' – family members and people living in the community.

During conversations I would hear older people saying proverbs for different scenarios in everyday life. These proverbs have stayed with me and these sayings have been passed down from generation to generation. I remember these sayings with fondness because they remind me of the wise words elderly people would say. I hope some of them will make you think or make you smile.

Saying: Moon will run until day catches it.
Meaning: The sun will rise then it will set and another day will begin.

Saying: The longest hedgerow must come to an end.
Meaning: The journey might seem long but it will come to an end.

Saying: Behind every dark cloud, there is a silver lining.
Meaning: If you feel disappointed, some good will come your way.

Saying: The father has eaten some sour grapes and the children's teeth are set on edge.
Meaning: If a father does bad things his kids will do the same bad things.

Saying: Tomorrow, the sun might never shine.
Meaning: Perhaps you are feeling a little sorry for yourself, you must remember that tomorrow is another day.

Saying: With each disappointment, there is a blessing.
Meaning: Perhaps you are disappointed but good things will happen.

Saying: The higher the monkey climbs, the more he will expose himself.
Meaning: The more a person shows off, the more they will get caught.

Saying: No fishmonger will tell you that his fish stink.
Meaning: A person will lie to protect their own interests.

Saying: Cat luck ain't dog one.
Meaning: Not everyone has the same luck.

Saying: One half of a loaf is better than none.
Meaning: It is better to have a job with less money than to have nothing at all.

Saying: Ease your hand out of the lion's mouth.
Meaning: You have a dispute with a person and you slowly step away.

Saying: Nothing can never happen before its time.
Meaning: It could be a wedding, a birth, or something great – it will happen at the right time.

Saying: Remember not to bite the hand that feeds you.
Meaning: Be kind to the person who has helped you in the past.

Saying: Burnt children must stand clear of fire.
Meaning: You've been in trouble once so you must stay away from trouble again.

Saying: Your eyes are too large/or too big.
Meaning: You must not covet other people's things.

Saying: The mauby lady say: who taste it – know it (Mauby is a Bajan soft drink).
Meaning: If you've experienced something, you'll understand how it feels.

Saying: What do not catch you; do not pass you.
Meaning: You must not rejoice on someone else's misfortune because it might be your turn next.

Saying: Every bar pig will have its day.
Meaning: Do not be hasty to laugh at others' mistakes.

Saying: The same tongue which bless you today might curse you the next.
Meaning: One day someone will be nice to you and the next day they could say something hurtful.

Saying: When your own dog bite you, you are properly bitten.

Meaning: When someone from your friendship or family circle is mean to you – you have been wronged in a severe way.

Saying: You throw sprats to catch mackerel.

Meaning: You are hearing some gossip, so you will continue to keep the conversation going to learn more.

Saying: If greedy wait, hot will cool.

Meaning: What's your hurry, you must take your time.

Saying: Two head bulls cannot reign in the same cattle pen.

Meaning: Two strong personalities cannot get along in the same house/area/environment.

Saying: Where money won't get you, manners will.

Meaning: Even though you may have no money, good manners will get you far in life.

Saying: Feed that person with a long spoon.

Meaning: If you don't trust someone, avoid telling them too much and keep them at a distance.

Saying: You can hide and buy ground but you can't hide and work it.

Meaning: You cannot keep a secret forever.

Saying: You might pull out the nail but the hole is still there.
Meaning: You may move on from trouble, but the hurt still remains.

Saying: Bad news, don't lack a carrier.
Meaning: Bad news travels fast.

Saying: High wind knows where to find an old house.
Meaning: If two people have a disagreement and gossip spreads – the person will go and find the gossiper to tell them off.

Saying: Every saucepan has its lid.
Meaning: There is a romantic match/mate to fit every person.

Saying: Girl – ya pot don't have no lid.
Meaning: You often get the blame or you're falsely accused.

Saying: Those who God bless, let no man curse.
Meaning: It doesn't matter what people might say – you are blessed by God.

Acknowledgements

With heartfelt thanks.

There are so many people I could name who have played a special part in my life throughout the years as a source of help and spiritual guidance.

I wish I could name all of you but here are a few names: Alrick Cummings, Winnie Cummings, Mavis Alleyne, Elizabeth Carter, David Geary, John Frew, Rev John Stephens and John Coleman.